GOSPEL THEMES:
Four Portraits of Christ's Life

Jim Townsend

DAVID C. COOK PUBLISHING CO.
ELGIN, ILLINOIS • WESTON, ONTARIO

To Steve Board, a modern Barnabas—
encourager of many.

Gospel Themes: Four Portraits of Christ's Life
© 1987 by David C. Cook Publishing Co.

David C. Cook Publishing Co., 850 North Grove Avenue, Elgin, IL 60120, Printed in U.S.A.

Editor: Gary Wilde
Designer: Dawn Lauck
Cover: Bakstad Photographics

ISBN:1-55513-848-9
Library of Congress Catalog Number:87-70312

CONTENTS

INTRODUCTION

Welcome to the Bible Mastery Series, designed to aid serious Bible students in group settings. Ideally, every student should have a copy of this study manual. Then the group sessions will be spent focusing largely upon the questions and activities at the back of the book in the DIRECTIONS FOR GROUP LEADERS section, p. 128. **Since all participants should have read the up-front commentary before class, the group's time can be spent primarily upon sharing experiences about how to apply these truths to their lives (rather than in factual and interpretive discussions).**

Each chapter contains many quotes and ideas from the best of past and present evangelical scholarship. In effect, I have provided a mini-library of information from the standard, solid commentators that Bible students will turn to for interpretation and explanation. In most cases, the Notes section at the back of the book will give sources for the information. I did the digging, you get the results!

The Symbols

Various boxes are set off from the rest of the text. These will give background information or illustration from such areas as theology, archaeology, original languages, etc. Here is a key to the symbols:

 GREEKSPEAK: Concise explanations of important Greek words, tenses, syntax, to help with interpreting the text's meaning.

 THEOLOGITALK: Discusses theological terms and doctrinal issues in relation to the text.

 CAN YOU DIG IT? Gives valuable cultural insight from archaeology.

 QUOTABLE QUOTES: Memorable statements from various sources.

 WINDOW ON THE WORD: Anecdotal material to illustrate a point in the text.

 THOUGHT QUESTION: A chance to pause and reflect on issues raised in the text.

Imagine four famous painters. Let's imagine we're talking about each of these artists as having painted essentially the same scene. First, there's Monet with the Impressionist's version, as if he had used small bird feathers for paint. At least, that's how it looks to a novice from a distance. Van Gogh's version of the same scene might look to a child as if he had painted on the canvas many long worms lying side by side. Leonardo da Vinci might make the conservative art viewer feel that he is back in the realm of reality—with more lifelike-looking dimensions. In other words, the painting is looking increasingly like a photograph. Then, for a fourth view we might select a more bizarre modernist version of the same scene. Four literary painters interpreting the same subject—that's what we find in our Gospels. Consequently, while we see great areas of overlap in the Gospels, we are also able to distinguish the earmarks of the individual writers in their art of historical treatment.

This book is devoted to exploring the major distinguishing themes of each of the four Gospels. Its purpose it to help you have a keener sense of the uniquenesses characterizing Matthew, Mark, Luke, and John.

Ready.

Set.

Go!

CHAPTER

1

GOSPEL ON THE GO

Characteristics of Mark

It's the age of brown 'n' serve, heat 'n' eat, chill 'n' pour. We live in a hurry, scurry, flurry, and worry era. It's the commuter and computer generation. In short, it's a time of instants. What once took an oven an hour to cook takes a microwave a matter of instants. What once took a secretary 15 minutes to type can be Xeroxed in instants. Instants seem to be the one constant of a technological people.

Perhaps even the unknown Christian poet was whisked off his feet by this breathtaking pace as he wrote:

> I have only just a minute,
> > Only sixty seconds in it.
> Forced upon me—can't refuse it;
> > Didn't seek it, didn't choose it.
> I must suffer if I lose it,
> > Give account if I abuse it.
> I have only just a minute,
> > But eternity is in it!

Yes, eternity intersected time in the person of Jesus Christ. That is the marrow of Mark's message.

For each of the four Gospels you will be supplied with a succinct sentence encapsuling the essence of each gospel for memorizing:

Memorize: **Mark is an action-packed gospel for Roman readers, about the serving Son of God, bearing Peter's stamp.**

The four fundamental features that are the focus of lessons 1 and 2 are these:

1) an action-packed gospel;

2) for Roman readers;

3) about the serving Son of God;

4) bearing Peter's stamp.

Get ready! Get set! Charge into the study!

I. An Action-packed Gospel

Have you ever watched old home movies where, say, a softball game is being photographed? On camera you see the amateur slugger step up to the plate and uncork a blast to the far reaches of the outfield. About halfway down the first base line the cameraman loses his featured runner. From then on the fans at home watch the camera chasing a cloud of dust around the base paths. As the runner slides into home plate and the umpire flings his arms out wide, the camera finally catches up with the action. This on-the-run pace is something like our first major feature of Mark's Gospel. Mark is a fast-paced, action-packed gospel. It is the gospel for the activist and adventurer.

Below are listed seven characteristics that show why Mark is such an action-packed gospel.

A. The "Shortie." In brief, Mark is the briefest of all four Gospels. Naturally, therefore, he must cram as much adventure into his compact story as possible.

B. His Favorite "Immediately"'s. The little adverb "immediately" (Greek: *euthus* [you-THOOSE]), or "straightway" in the King James Version, is used 42 times in Mark's Gospel. This is a significant statistic because that amount is more frequent than in all the rest of the New Testament put together! By means of this little "immediately," or "at once," Mark gallops while others lope along at a slower pace. For examples, see Mark 1:12, 18, 43.

C. "And . . . And . . . And." Have you ever heard a small child telling excitedly about something amazing that just happened? She narrates the adventure with 'n'-ies—"'n he was the bad guy runnin' 'n he jumped into his car 'n he started to chase him 'n he . . ."

In childlike fashion, Mark had the "'n"-ies. Some 400 times in this shortest of the four Gospels (as over against 250 times in the much longer Matthew and 380 in Luke) Mark grabs up his word "and." In the KJV of Mark 3, 27 of the 35 verses begin with "and." In fact, in the four verses of Mark 8:6-9, "and" appears 13 times in the Authorized Version. "And" is like one of the firing pistons in Mark's engine.

D. The Historical Present. Sometimes for literary effect a writer who is writing about the past will use a present tense in telling the story.

This gives the narrative a more on-the-spot, lifelike effect. For instance, "Caesar crosses the Rubican and his soldiers are plunging into the waters," etc. Luke only uses this effect one time (!) and Matthew 21 times. But with Mark it's a fad—or, rather, hallmark of his gospel. He uses it about 150 times.

E. Verbs with Verve. Had Mark been a hyperactive child? You get the feeling that he couldn't sit still very long. Many commentators feel that the tantalizing vignette Mark included in Mark 14:51, 52 of a "young man" in the Garden of Gethsemane who "fled . . . leaving his garment behind" is in all probability a pen photo of the author himself. Even then, Mark was on the run.

Notice these other examples of running or rapid movement in Mark:
  (1) The rich young ruler "*ran* up to" Jesus (10:17);
  (2) Blind Bartimaeus threw his cloak aside, "*jumped* to his feet and came to Jesus" (10:50);
  (3) "The women . . . *fled* from the tomb" (16:8);
  (4) And by contrast, at Christ's tomb we finally encounter an angelic "young man . . . in a white robe *sitting*" (16:5).

It is as if, having seen Christ risen, one can finally heave a sigh of relief. Of course, one might still run out to tell others! Because of its running narrative, Mark ought to be called the Jogger's Gospel.

F. Missing Matters Bureau. Activists are omitters. If you're going to get on with it, you're going to have to get rid of some things. Therefore, in order to keep pace, Mark must eliminate some matters that otherwise might be told.

As we hop into Mark's compact model, we notice (by comparison with Matthew 1 and 2 as well as Luke 1 and 2) that the stories about Jesus' birth are nonexistent at the front door of Mark's Gospel. Furthermore, the ending seems as abrupt as its beginning. (Most orthodox scholars hold that the original Greek text of Mark 16 only extends through verse 8.)

G. Doing Versus Teaching. One of the major reasons for the preceding point is that while Matthew incorporates five massive units of Jesus' teaching and Luke includes many memorable parables, Mark virtually eliminates the Savior's sermons (except for chapters 4 and 13). Mark tends to tell us *that* Jesus taught rather than *what* He taught. By one count, "Mark gives only four of the parables of Jesus, while Matthew has fifteen and Luke nineteen. There is no Sermon on the Mount in Mark. In Matthew's mission instruction to the disciples (10:5-42) there are 38 verses, whereas Mark compresses the incident into four verses in 6:8-11.

The following chart from Harold St. John[1] illustrates the estimate of differences between action and teaching in the four Gospels.

	Mark	Matthew	Luke	John
Narrative	45%	25%	34%	16%
Teaching	55%	75%	66%	84%

Exposition, then, gives way to events in Mark's action-packed gospel.

Yes, Mark's Gospel joggles like a Model-T Ford on a pitted, gravel country road or like a herky-jerky Charlie Chaplin movie. All the more reason that Mark's Gospel with its panting penmanship is tailored to today. It is the gospel for lawyers with their briefcases, get-the-job-done consultants, housewives taxiing kids to little league and soccer, schedule-conscious, calendar-carrying executives. For the hustle and bustle of modern megalopolis living, on the Mark, get set, go!

II. Audience: For Roman Readers

Modern marketers test the publishing waters before taking the product plunge. They want their published products to fill the niche of Joe and Joanna Consumer's perceived need. Consequently, they don't use polysyllabic words in childrens' books or put "Run, Mac, run" books in college bookstores.

Mark did something similar. Mark's Gospel is an audience-adapted book. It is generally held that it was written for Roman readers. (Repeat the single sentence you memorized on Mark.)

YOUR AVERAGE ROMAN READER

 What picture do you have of Roman readers? What qualities do you think would appeal to them? What qualities in Jesus would appeal to the people in your neighborhood and workplace?

Romans were the movers and shakers of their day. The entire New Testament is couched within the context of the Roman Empire. As a rule, Romans were concerned with conquest rather than contemplation. Consequently, Mark's message need not be embellished with excessive embroidery. "Just get us the facts fast!"—that would be the emphasis. As a result, Mark's message must be gauged to worker and warrior.

What are the giveaway clues in Mark's Gospel that demonstrate that he was writing with his mind tuned in to the Roman channel and character? In answer to that question, we might consider the following:

A. Christ as Controversial Conqueror. Jesus is presented in Mark's Gospel as serving Son of God (10:45; 1:1). Since this will be the subject matter for lesson 2 of this study guide, we will say no more about it here.

B. Christ the Controversialist. What type of character would appeal to a Roman centurion? Probably someone who was made of sterling mettle and unafraid of conflict would elicit a positive response from Romans.

In Mark 2:1—3:6, the author gives us a pen sketch of Christ the controversialist—undaunted by criticism and unafraid of conflict. Mark 2:1—3:6 is a clustering of five run-ins Jesus had with religious rulers. Scholars call these "conflict stories." Here we meet Jesus the Wrecker—the embarrassing Jesus.

2:1-12 Paralyzed man through the roof
2:13-17 Eating with Levi
2:18-22 Fasting versus feasting
2:23-28 Sabbath controversy
3:1-6 Man with withered hand healed in synagogue

In the chart provided below fill in the items called for in each case.

	Specific opponent	Cause of conflict	Christ's response	Lesson I learn
2:1-12				
2:13-17				

11

	Specific opponent	Cause of conflict	Christ's response	Lesson I learn
2:18-22				
2:23-28				
3:1-6				

? How do you think Jesus would have rated here on winning friends and influencing people (a la Dale Carnegie)? Is it proper for Christians ever to be upsetting, upset upsetters?

C. Activists Love Action. The animated, nonstop writing style would be in line with our stereotype of the Roman mentality. Even in the closing comment of Mark 16:20, as the disciples actively worked, "the Lord worked with them."

D. Latinisms. If Mark were writing to "Nero-ville" (Rome), we would expect overtones of the Latin language to burst through at points. For example, if a comedian should say, "Whatsa mattah wit you, my little bambino?"—we would hear the Italian style being caricatured behind the English words. Even so, Mark's Gospel is full of Latinisms—more than in any other New Testament book. Just as *piano* is a word carried over into English from Italian, so also Mark's vocabulary is punctuated with numerous words carried over into Greek from Latin.

? What words can you think of that have been brought over wholesale from some foreign language into English?

Below are listed some of the Latinisms embedded in the Greek text of Mark's Gospel:
- pallet or camp bed (2:4, 9, 11);
- *modius* for "bowl" (4:21);

- legion (5:9, 15), i.e., over 6000 Roman soldiers;
- "executioner" (6:27; *speculator* in Greek), "one of the bodyguard" (JB);
- *sextarius* (7:4), or "pitcher" for measuring liquids (only here in the New Testament);
- *census* (12:14), or "taxes to Caesar";
- "small copper coins" or *quadrans* (12:42);
- "centurion" (15:39, 44).

Obviously, most of these items have to do with Roman money, measurements, and military matters.

E. Aramaisms. This point is much like the reverse side of the coin of the previous point. Not only in a presentation to Roman readers might we expect some leftover Latin, but we might also find some hangovers from the original language spoken by Jesus and His disciples. It is commonly agreed that Jesus used the spoken language then common in Palestine, namely, Aramaic.

A number of Aramaic fragments, carry over into the text of Mark's Gospel, generally regarded as the earliest Gospel. Consequently, each of these terms is translated for the Roman readers. Below is a list of some:

- "Boanerges, which means Sons of Thunder," (3:17);
- " 'Talitha koum!' (which means 'Little girl . . . get up!')" (5:41);
- " 'Corban' (that is, a gift devoted to God)" (7:11);
- " 'Ephphatha!' (which means, 'Be opened')" (7:34);
- "Abba [meaning] Father" (14:36);
- " 'Eloi, Eloi, lama sabachthani?'—which means, 'My God, my God, why have you forsaken me?' " (15:34).

When we hear "IRA," "interest," "deductions," etc., we know that we have entered the technical world of money matters. Even so, the six terms above take us into the back room conversations, so to speak, of Jesus and His disciples. Presumably this wording was handed down via Jesus through Peter (on the scene) to Mark. Thus, in Mark 5:41, with the raising of Jairus's daughter, Jesus had probably used the same "time to wake up" type words that she had been awakened by all her life.

F. Say What? We have the saying, "When in Rome, do as the Romans do." But, assuming that Mark is writing to Romans, we would expect him to explain to them those things that they do not ever do in Rome. Consequently, we discover these tipoffs in Mark's Gospel. For one thing, Mark never once uses that word so fond to Jesus—"law." If he had, Roman law could have been easily confused with Jewish law. Mark has "fewer Old Testament quotations and allusions than have Matthew and Luke, about 63, as against about 128 in Matthew, and between 90 and 100 in Luke."[2] Furthermore, this feature accounts for the amplified explanation of the Jews' ceremonial washings in Mark in Mark 7:3-16.

G. Note Dropping. Throughout Mark's Gospel are sprinkled notes of the sort that we might expect to find if Mark was writing to Rome. For instance, why does Mark include at 1:13 a note not found in any other Gospel? Mark notes that in His temptation, Jesus was "with the wild animals." Such information might be encouraging to Christians in Rome—those who might some day have to face wild animals in the arena!

In Mark 10:12 we find an addition (not found in Matthew with its Jewish orientation). Why? It makes sense in light of the fact that Jewish women could not divorce their husbands but Roman women could.

Mark 15:21 contains a detail not found in the other three Gospels—that Simon of Cyrene was "the father of Alexander and Rufus." What point would there be to including this item unless it was relevant to the Roman readers? Interestingly, in Romans 16:13 we meet a Rufus—presumably the same person. Those two may have become quite well known in the Christian community before this gospel was written.

III. About the Serving Son of God

(Note: We will spend a whole chapter on this subject: see Lesson 2.)

IV. Author and Apostle: Bearing Peter's Stamp

Repeat your single sentence you have memorized on Mark's Gospel, with the phrase "bearing Peter's stamp." It is generally agreed that the author, John Mark, and his gospel seem stamped with the imprint of the irrepressible apostle Peter. Of the four Gospel writers, neither Mark nor Luke were apostles. Nevertheless, it appears that:

> Mark bears Peter's stamp, and
> Luke bears Paul's stamp.

It is as if there are apostles standing in the shadows behind both books.

Biofeedback on Mark

Let's get a brief bit of biography on John Mark, whose Jewish name was John and whose Latin name was Marcus. Consider these points:

1. In that curiosity-rousing cameo before the Crucifixion, it would

seem logical that the "young man who . . . fled naked" from the arrest scene in the garden (Mk. 14:51, 52) must have been the author, Mark. Mark was probably ten years younger than the apostles, or about 20 years old when Jesus was crucified.

2. Mark's home was apparently home base for a strategic section of the Jerusalem church (Acts 12:12). Probably his mother was a well-to-do widow, for the "outer entrance" of her house's architecture and employment of a "servant girl" (Acts 12:12) both suggest a specific social status.

3. Barnabas was Mark's cousin (Col. 4:10), so it was natural to take Mark on the First Missionary Journey (about A.D. 47-49) as their "assistant" (Acts 13:5; LB). Mark was a kind of "missionary in training"—an apprentice, or understudy.

4. Acts 13:13 introduces us to Mark the defector. Why he went A.W.O.L. is unexplained. Suggested reasons for his return are: being a victim of malarial mosquitoes, fear of the robber-infested territory, irritation at his cousin Barnabas's being displaced by Paul as main leader on the mission, homesickness, questions about Gentiles and the Gospel.

APOSTLES UNGLAMORIZED

5. The top of the volcano comes off in Acts 15:36-41. Paul proposed a second missionary trip, and Barnabas proposed that Mark go along. Result: explosion (15:39).

6. Multiplied missions resulted from the blow-up between two missionaries. Paul took Silas, and "Barnabas took Mark and sailed for Cyprus" (15:39).

7. For 11 or 12 years after the split-up, we read nothing in Scripture about Mark's activities.

8. References from Rome—most probably—during Paul's second imprisonment (about A.D. 67) provide us with Paul's revised version of John Mark.

? How is Mark's spiritual safari a form of encouragement to us all?

Mark is a paradigm of restoration. His parabolic pathway teaches us that failure need not be final. "We may be knocked down but we are never knocked out!" (II Cor. 4:9, J. B. Philips). Don't despair! Siphon strength from the mistake made by Mark and the revised version of him by Paul.

Peter's Penman

Not only did Mark have a loyal cousin in Barnabas, but evidently he had a spiritual father in Peter. Peter dubbed Mark "my son" (I Pet. 5:13). Probably this means that Mark was a Christian convert of Peter's.

As a matter of fact, there are at least seven early church fathers (that is, major Christian leaders after the time of the apostles) who show that Peter had a profound influence upon Mark's message. Parodying the senior Isaac's comment to deceptive Jacob in Genesis 27:22, someone has well said of this Gospel that the hand that transcribed it is the hand of Mark, but the voice is the voice of Peter.

MARK AND WE MODERNS

For folks whose life gears keep meshing with the feverish pitch of a computer printout, Mark still speaks. The Booklet of Mark has the same purpose as the engraved hymn line at the base of Charles Wesley's statue in Bristol, England—which reads; "O let me commend my Savior to you." Consider the claims of this controversial Christ. We must not, said Dorothy Sayers, pare down the claws of the Lion of the tribe of Judah, Jesus. Like Aslan the Lion in C. S. Lewis's Narnia series, the strong Son of God must be confronted in all His fierce majesty.

> What will you do with Jesus?
> Neutral you cannot be.
> One day your heart will be asking,
> What will He do with me?

CHAPTER
2

WHO AM I?
Mark's Mystery Man

MAJOR TITLES OF CHRIST

Poet Richard Watson Gilder avowed:

> If Jesus Christ is a man,—
> And only man,—I say
> That of all mankind I cleave to him,
> And to Him will I cleave alway.
> If Jesus Christ is God,—
> And the only God,—I swear
> I will follow Him through heaven and hell,
> The earth, the sea, and the air!

Was the poet accurate in his appraisal? Did he depict a Biblical Jesus? The poem seems to say that one could discard one or the other of Jesus' classifications ("man . . . God") and He would still be worthy of an all-out following. Is that true?

Benjamin Franklin once wrote in a letter to the president of Yale: "As to Jesus of Nazareth, . . . I have . . . some doubts as to his Divinity, tho' it is a question I do not dogmatize upon, having never studied it . . . ."[1] Is Jesus deity (or God), as Richard Watson Gilder allowed as a possibility?

In this lesson we will undertake a study of TWO MAJOR TITLES OF CHRIST as they relate to His character in Matthew, Mark, and Luke: The Son of God and the Servant of the Lord. While both titles or ideas are found outside of Mark (and for this reason this lesson also includes Bible references outside of Mark), they are pivotal to Mark's Gospel and so will be studied here.

THE SON OF GOD

On the doorstep of Mark's Gospel, we are introduced to "the gospel about Jesus Christ, the Son of God" (1:1). Although this last title is not found in a few of the ancient Greek manuscripts at Mark 1:1, it is found in a number of important early manuscripts. Therefore, it is a part of the translation of the ASV, RSV, NEB, JB, etc., at Mark 1:1. In fact, it seems to serve as a kind of centerpiece for the mantle of Mark's Gospel. (Repeat at this point your memorized capsule sentence from the last chapter.)

I might say to an immigrant just arrived from Africa or Laos, "Do you want to go to the county fair?" However, even if the individual could speak English, but he had never seen or heard of a "county fair," he would not know what I meant by the expression. All communication depends upon a common deposit of shared ideas and words. Consequently, we must explore the world of words in that time in order to figure out how these crucial titles of Jesus were being used.

I. Varied Biblical Usages

The title "sons of God" is used in a number of ways within the Bible itself. Below we survey some major ways in which this title is used. It is used for:

A. Angels. It is widely agreed that in verses like Job 1:6 and 2:1 the title "sons of God" refers to angels. The NIV even translates "sons of God" there as "angels."

B. Created, Human Offspring. Although the specific title "sons of God" is not used in the Bible for all human beings, it would seem proper to understand it in that sense from Malachi 2:10 and Acts 17:29 ("God's offspring"). Malachi 2:10 asks in parallel poetry:

> Have we not all one Father?
> Did not one God create us?

If God is the Father who created us all, then it is implied that human beings are sons of God by creation. (That, however, does not mean that all human beings are approved in their relationship with God; see John 8:42-44.)

C. Israel As a Nation. In Exodus 4:22 the Lord says, "Israel is my firstborn son."

D. Israel's King As the People's Representative. Ultimately II Samuel 7:12-14 points on to David's greater Son (Jesus), but more immediately II Samuel 7:14a pronounces: "I will be his father, and he will be my son." (Note that 7:14b assumes the individual referred to will do wrong, so Christ cannot be the complete point of reference.)

18

E. God's Regenerated Children. In John's Gospel the Greek word for "Son" is reserved exclusively for Jesus, whereas reborn humans are properly called the "children of God" (Jn. 1:12, 13). Not all Bible writers, however, subscribe to this same usage. Paul wrote to Christians in Galatians 3:26—"You are all sons of God through faith in Christ Jesus." Thus, we become sons of God by believing in *the* Son of God.

F. The Mysterious Suggestion. The Old Testament does not overtly teach a doctrine of the Trinity. However, within the room dimensions occupied by God in the Old Testament, so to speak, there is left sufficient space to fill in that room with the later furniture of a New Testament teaching on the subject. For instance, below is a tantalizing text from Proverbs 30:4 (printed from the NEB), that enlivens the pulse of any Christian.

> Who has ever gone up to heaven and come down again?
>> Who has cupped the wind in the hollow of his hands?
> Who has bound up the waters in the fold of his garment?
>> Who has fixed the boundaries of the earth?
> What is his name or *his son's name,* if you know it?

II. Jewish Literature Outside of the Bible

Jews didn't just stop talking about God and other spiritual topics for the 400-plus so-called "Silent Years" between Malachi and Matthew. There was a body of religious literature developing then, although the Jews never officially made it a part of their sacred Scriptures.

The title "Son of God" appears "in only one passage before the first century. In the fifth book of Enoch, God says, 'For I and my Son will be united with them forever' (En. 105:2)."[2] Another one of the scant references outside the Bible is found in the Apocryphal II Esdras 2:47: "He answered and said to me [concerning one who crowned a great multitude of the immortal on Mount Zion], 'He is the Son of God, whom they confessed in the world.' " This latter sounds like an excerpt hoisted right out of John's Epistles.

III. Other Literature Outside of the Bible

A. Hellenistic (i.e., Greek-speaking) wonder workers were called "divine men" or "sons of God."

B. Alexander the Great had been called by Egyptian priests (probably to save their skins) a "son of the god."

C. Greek and Roman myths told of the "sons of the gods" who had sexual relations with mortal women.

D. The Roman emperor was called "divine" and the "son of god."

19

IV. New Testament Strategic Spots

A. Mark's Thematic Take-off (Mk. 1:1). George Ladd observed that "in the Synoptics (i.e., Matthew, Mark, and Luke), Jesus never uses the full title the *Son of God* to designate himself; but he frequently refers to himself as the Son."[3] However, many people within the Gospels do speak of Jesus as "the Son of God." It would appear to be the launching pad for the Gospel of Mark. This conquering champion commended to the Roman reader is the superhuman Son of God.

B. Jesus' Baptism (Mk. 1:11). As Jesus came up out of the baptismal water, God's great audiovisual imprimatur came down upon Him. Both the visual symbol of the Spirit as dove and the voice of God the Father combined to serve notice:

> You are my Son, whom I love;
> with you I am well pleased.

It was as if God had pasted together Psalm 2:7 and Isaiah 42:1 (we will say more about this under the title "servant").

No New Testament writer comes right out and says, "Now let me explain for you the exact significance of Jesus' baptism." However, there are at least five flashes of meaning that we can glean from various verses that help to show its significance.

1. It was a kind of coronation ceremony. Note the parallelism in the chart below.

I SAMUEL 16:13	MARK 1:10
Samuel anointed David	Jesus = the Anointed One (or Christ)
"From that day the Spirit of the Lord came upon David in power"	"The Spirit descending on him like a dove"
David's official kinging	Therefore . . . .

2. It marked the manifestion of Messiah's public ministry and served as the identifying factor for John the Baptist (Jn. 1:31-33).

3. It was "proper . . . to fulfill all righteousness" (Mt. 3:15).

4. It identified the Sinless One with repentant sinners.

5. It identified Him as the Servant of Isaiah (42:1).

C. Jesus' Temptation (Mt. 4:1-11). Graham Scroggie said of the sequence of Jesus' temptations following His baptism: "After the dove, the devil; after the testimony, the test."

? What does this rhythmic sequence in Jesus' life teach us about what we might expect in the Christian life pattern?

After God proclaimed, "This is my Son" (Mt. 3:17), the Devil countered, "If you are the Son of God . . ." (Mt. 4:3, 6). After being divinely attested, He was diabolically tested.

D. Nathanael's Confession (Jn. 1:49). Andrew informed his brother Simon, "We have found the Messiah" (Jn. 1:41). Philip informed Nathanael, "We have found the one Moses wrote about in the Law, and about whom the prophets also wrote" (Jn. 1:45), thereby defining more fully the meaning of Messiah. Nathanael's own confession was:

> You are the Son of God;
> you are the King of Israel" (Jn. 1:49).

E. Underworld Confession (Mk. 3:11). Even the "evil spirits" (or demons) designated Him, "You are the Son of God." Here in Mark 3:11 the supernatural evil beings recognize the supernatural Son.

F. Walking on Water (Mt. 14:33). The astonished disciples worshiped Him, saying, "Truly you are the Son of God."

G. The Climactic Confession (Mt. 16:16). Note in the chart below the pivotal points at which Jesus' deity is declared.

Angel's Announcement	Climactic Confession	Transfiguration	Crucifixion
Lk. 1:35	Mt. 16:16	Mk. 9:7	Mk. 15:39
"The holy one to be born will be called the Son of God."	"You are the Christ, the Son of the living God."	"This is my Son, whom I love."	"Surely this man was the Son of God."

H. Jesus' Transfiguration (Mk. 9:7; Mt. 17:5; Lk. 9:35). Alfred Edersheim wrote that as "His question, like Moses' rod, struck their hearts, there leaped from the lips of Peter the living, life-spreading waters of his confession."[4] Just after it seemed "like a million floodlights were turned on inside Him" (*Looking Ahead*, David C. Cook), the divine voice proclaimed, "This is my Son" (Mk. 9:7).

I. The John-like Outcropping (Mt. 11:25-27; Lk. 10:21, 22). George Ladd called these verses "the most important passage for the study of the Synoptic Christology [i.e., the study of Christ]."[5] It has been called a "Johannine Thunderbolt" for it seems to intrude into the Synoptic Gospels with language that sounds like it was hoisted wholesale out of John's Gospel. "Even the Gospel of John contains nothing which penetrates more deeply into the essential relation of the Son to the Father."[6]

J. The Vineyard Parable (Mk. 12:6). In the allegory of the violent tenants—after the owner (representing the Father) mercifully sends numerous installments of servants to the tenant farmers—the owner says climactically, "They will respect my son" (Mk. 12:6), but the tenants killed the son in the story, prefiguring the death of God's Son.

K. The "Ignorant Son" (Mk. 13:32). Here we are introduced to a profound mystery about the person of Jesus—in His disclaimer about not knowing the time of the Second Coming.

L. The Centurion's Confession (Mk. 15:39). The centurion had undoubtedly heard the contemptuous crucifixion crowd take up the taunting title (Mt. 27:40). However, we must not necessarily overload the centurion's title with our later orthodox meaning, for in his parallel account Luke has said, "Surely this was a righteous man" (Lk. 23:47). Even though the Roman centurion may not have had his boxcar of thought laden with the same cargo that we might, his exclamation still supports the claims of Mark that "this man was the Son of God" in the full-orbed sense meant by Mark (15:39).

M. God's P.A. System (Rom. 1:3, 4). Although this passage is outside the Gospels, we include it here to show how Paul—writing perhaps to some of the same Romans as Mark—conceived of the term. Writing less than 30 years after Jesus was impaled upon what Cicero called "the most cruel and hideous of punishments," an arch-Jew and former assassin of Christians could assert that God's Good News revolves around God's "Son who as to his human nature was a descendant of David, and who through the Spirit of holiness was declared with power to be the Son of God by his resurrection."

Jesus is Son-of-God-with-power. How so? By His resurrection. His resurrection is God's P.A. system broadcasting the truth about Jesus' person. The resurrection didn't make Jesus something new. It communicated clearly what He already was—God's Son.

SERVANT OF THE LORD

Repeat your memory sentence. We called Jesus "the serving Son of God." While on earth Jesus fulfilled the role carried out in Isaiah's "Servant of the Lord." To understand this concept that so controlled Christ's career, we must briefly study the background in Isaiah.

I. Isaiah's 'Servant of the Lord'

Throughout the latter half of Isaiah are sprinkled snippets and portraits of a "Servant of the Lord." Frequently, conservative Protestants have immediately yelled, "That's Jesus." By contrast, many modern Jews view Isaiah's servant as the suffering nation of Israel. However, the fact is that this servant is a complex concept. In other words, *we cannot exhaust the identity of Isaiah's servant with a single identification.* Let's look at some of the possibilities:

A. The Servant = Israel. Unquestionably, on occasion in Isaiah the servant is identified as Israel. Check Isaiah 41:8 ("Israel, my servant"); 44:21 ("my servant, O Israel"); 48:20b ("The Lord . . . his servant Jacob"). However, other passages cause us to ask: Is the Servant of the Lord concept exhausted by the identity of Israel? The answer is no.

B. Beyond Israel. In Isaiah 49:6 the servant has a mission *to* Israel. In Isaiah 53:4-6, 11, and 12 the servant suffers *for* Israel. Therefore, Israel is exempted from providing the total identity of the Servant of the Lord.

C. Servant Songs of Isaiah. There are at least four sections in Isaiah that provide an expanded portrait of the servant—42:1-4; 49:1-6; 50:4-9; and 52:13—53:12. Filter from these four passages some of the characteristics of the Servant. Write your findings here:

_____

_____

_____

_____

_____

_____

_____

_____

Alfred Edersheim has a helpful diagram to put the identity of the servant in perspective—the servant is, one might say, a multiple personality (including Israel in some cases, but not exhausted by Israel).

MESSIAH

REMNANT OF TRUE ISRAEL

ALL ISRAEL

This composite personality profile matches the complex picture of the Servant of the Lord in the data of Isaiah.

II. New Testament References

Now let's survey the major New Testament passages highlighting the mission of Jesus as Servant of the Lord. Actually, that title is not directly used of Him in the King James Version, although the NIV, RSV, NEB, etc., will use "servant" in Acts 3:13, 26 and 4:27, 30. This translation is preferable to the KJV's "Son" or "child." This is because the same Greek word (*pais*), found four times in Acts, is used to render the Hebrew "servant" in Isaiah 52:13 of the Septuagint (the Greek translation of the Hebrew Old Testament generally used by the apostles).

A. Mark 1:11. This is an easy one to miss "unless someone explains it" (Acts 8:31). At Jesus' baptism a voice came from heaven:

> You are my Son, whom I love;
> with you I am well pleased.

A mule is a hybrid between a horse and a donkey. Even so, the divinely spoken imprimatur, or seal of approval, upon Jesus was a hybrid of two Old Testament verses—Psalm 2:7 and Isaiah 42:1.

It is readily agreed that the first phrase ("You are my Son") is hoisted from a Messianic psalm. The nations in verses 1 and 2 of Psalm 2 rage "against the Lord and against his Anointed One" (another name for Messiah). This Messiah is "installed as my [i.e., God's] King" in verse 6. Immediately following comes the announcement: "You are my Son." While each Hebrew king might be thought of as God's son, the New Testament writers envision the verse as having ultimate fulfilment in Jesus (see Psalm 2:7 quoted in Acts 13:33).

The second half of the announcement at Jesus' baptism is a takeover from Isaiah 42:1. Remember that Isaiah 42:1-4 is one of the Servant Songs of Isaiah. It opens: "Here is my servant . . . my chosen one in whom I delight" (42:1). Most importantly, the phrase "in whom I delight" (though not the same in the Greek Septuagint) reflects the second phrase of the divine voice—"with you I am well pleased." More significantly, the God-pleasing servant of Isaiah is the one about whom Isaiah forecasted: "I will put my Spirit on him." That is in fact precisely what is occurring in Mark 1:11 (and its parallels). Therefore, this is God's identicard for His servant. Jesus is Isaiah's Servant of the Lord.

B. Matthew 8:16, 17. Matthew 8:17 quotes Isaiah 53:4 from the fourth Servant Song. Matthew saw in Jesus' healings a fulfilment of "He . . . carried our sorrows" from Isaiah 53:4.

C. Matthew 12:15-21. In another Matthew passage after Jesus

24

"healed all their sick" Jesus receded from the public limelight, fulfilling the servant passage of Isaiah 42:1-4—that He would not be a pushy, bulldozer sort of figure, but a servant.

D. Mark 10:45. This verse may be considered the key verse in Mark's Gospel. Although in Greek the title "servant" is not used, the idea is very much present. Consequently, F. F. Bruce even translates the verse as indicating that the Son of Man came "to be a servant."[7] In Mark, Jesus is the serving Son of God. (Repeat the capsule sentence you memorized.) The Son of Man (who is Servant) came "to give his life as a ransom for *many*." The "many" ransomed is an echoing chord from Isaiah 53:12 ("he bore the sin of *many*"). Indeed, notice how Mark 10:45 fits so snugly into the main thought of Isaiah 53.

E. John 12:37, 38. Another verse from the servant passage in Isaiah 53:1 is quoted in John 12:37, 38.

Am I a Servant?

John Alexander visited another country and observed a servant sitting out in the car waiting, with hunger, on his wealthy master who had gone into the restaurant to eat. Alexander observed that all romanticized notions of being a Christian servant fly out the window for Americans who actually observe the drudgery that any real servant goes through.

Wayne Lowe was a Sunday School superintendant. His church had just recently built a new church sanctuary—with glowing claims of how great everything would be once the cramped church moved into its new, larger facility. However, reality soon dawned. Rising attendance meant that there were two classes above and behind the new sanctuary balcony and one that could be heard within the sanctuary as it met out in the foyer. Naturally, all this noise created tension. And where do you go with complaints if you're a Sunday School teacher? Why, to the superintendant, of course. In his capacity as superintendant, Wayne caught a lot of flak. He had to take the heat. He had to serve as a burden bearer. The Sunday School superintendant (often like a school principal or complaint department person) frequently has to absorb other people's anger.

As God's Servant, Jesus took the heat for us. He bore our burdens (Mk. 10:45). He became a flak-taker for us. Like Benjamin Franklin's lightning rod, Jesus' cross became a lightning rod absorbing God's electricity attracted by our sin.

Bob Schneider was an occupational burn therapist in California. He was given the task of helping David Rothenberg get rehabilitated from third

25

degree burns. David was a 7-year-old boy whose father had tried to burn him to death in a motel room. When Bob Schneider began the therapy of bending the burned limbs of David, his mother arched her 5-foot-5-inch frame like an attack dog. She demanded that Schneider stop inflicting pain upon her child. Bob's task was to convince that mother that David would have to undergo a lot more hurting in order to get maximum help. It seemed cruel, but the many thank-you notes Schenider showed her that he had received from other previous burn patients partially equipped her to withstand the hurt David must undergo to get help.

Bob Schneider had a lot of anger vented at him. His job called upon him to hurt people in order to help them. Schneider was a servant. Am I willing to become that kind of a servant for the Servant *par excellence?*

CHAPTER
3

A WIDENESS IN GOD'S MERCY

Jewish and Universal Tensions in Matthew

I doubt that you had a category (at least, as approved by the school administration) in your high school yearbook that proclaimed an individual: "Most Likely Not To Be Liked." I suspect that a little later in life Matthew may have felt that he filled that category.

Matthew's other name was Levi. Levi was the name of the tribe in Israel from which the priestly class was drawn—and to whom the other Israelites gave. This New Testament Levi was one to whom others grudgingly gave. He was part of the despised JRS—Jewish Revenue Service. Thus, Matthew was regarded as riffraff by the average religious Jew.

Consequently, Matthew must have been a walking time bomb, full of tension. He was a pro-Roman Jew in a society of anti-Roman Jews. How would it feel to walk down the streets of Capernaum and have people sneer at you and shun you? Matthew knew. Yes, he was among those most likely not to be liked!

It was precisely this tension, however—of walking a tightrope between two worlds—that made him the ideal candidate to write the gospel he did. It was a gospel for Jews to receive the King of the Jews and go on to overcome racism and love people of all nations. This is the distinctive point of tension in Matthew—Jewish nationalism and Christian internationalism.

Memorize: **Matthew is the fullest gospel for Jewish readers with Old Testament atmosphere, containing five sections of Jesus' systematic teaching.**

The Marks of Matthew

Minted and engraved into the Gospel of Matthew are the marks of

Matthew the man. What telltale markings might we expect to find in a gospel transcribed by a former tax collector?

Interestingly, in three parallel Gospel accounts, both Mark (2:14) and Luke (5:27) call the chief character "Levi," while only Matthew calls himself "Matthew" (9:9). Matthew, meaning "gift of the Lord," may be the name that the Jewish Levi took after becoming a Christian. It is perhaps significant that a man who charged people fees daily would be called "gift."

Another thing we might expect to find in the Gospel of the money man is a vault of references to money—and we do. Graham Scroggie observed, "There is more frequent mention of money in this Gospel than in any of the others, and more and rarer coins are introduced. Mark refers to three coins only, and these the poorest, the 'mite,' the 'farthing,' and the 'penny.' Luke refers to the 'mite,' and the 'farthing,' and also to 'pounds'; but Matthew, who was in the habit of handling money refers to coins of the highest value at the time; to the 'talent,' for example, which was worth about sixty times as much as the 'pound.' "[1]

Just as if a modern numismatist had written a newspaper article and referred to certain rare coins, even so Matthew (in 17:24 and 27) causes us to hear the clink and roll of a number of dropped coins in his gospel.

Another interesting sidelight is that the ex-tax collector is the only one of the four Gospel writers to tell us the miracle story of the Temple tax (Mt. 17:24-27). Who more than Matthew would be impressed by the miracle of "the two-drachma tax" (Mt. 17:24) taken from a fish? Peter the former fisherman caught the fish, and Matthew the ex-tax collector recorded the tax miracle. Furthermore, it occurred on Matthew's old tax ground of Capernaum.

Matthew alone records the parable found in Matthew 18:21-35. The indebted servant in the parable owed money in the millions by modern standards ("ten thousand talents," 18:24) yet the same forgiven servant begrudged another servant of one-third of a year's salary! Matthew helps us understand that forgiveness is incalculable.

Yet another money story is embedded only in Matthew at 20:1-16. It's a story about God's pay rates, so to speak. By ordinary standards it doesn't seem fair. People get paid the same amount of money for working different amounts of time. Yet the paymaster in the parable didn't gyp anybody. The first batch of workers received exactly what they were hired for. It was sheer generosity on the part of the employer to provide the last workers with serendipitous grace. Undeservedly, the last were favored on a par with the first hired hands. Matthew must have been aware that the huge sin-tax against him had been dropped, just as the king had done in Matthew 18:27.

Also in Matthew 20 the "denarius" (vs. 2) is mentioned. It is impossible to calculate accurately denominations of Biblical money, for world money standards are continually in flux. The King James's "penny a day" (20:2) is far wide of the modern mark, for a denarius was the amount of pay the average farmhand would receive for one day's work. Thus, if you compute your own salary for one day, you come closer to figuring out the modern equivalent of a denarius.

? What items might serve as tokens or symbols of your job or the way in which you spend the bulk of your time? How might these influences filter into your Christian experience?

Even in Matthew 13:52 we hear words aligned with Matthew's vocation—for one "who brings out of his storeroom new treasures as well as old." No doubt, the tax collector used some shorthand system to jot down records of figures as he sat at his toll booth. If so, such a shorthand system would have come in handy for jotting down the Savior's sermons (e.g., the Sermon on the Mount).

Tax collectors must have kept detailed records. Who better than a vocational notetaker might have been selected to give us this favorite and fullest of gospels? Who better than a Jew under hire to Rome could have captured in his own psyche the tension of a gospel to Jews for the whole world?

Jewish Ingredients

Matthew is a gospel for Jewish readers. (Repeat the sentence on Matthew you have memorized.) Yet we must not make a force fit out of any of the Gospels—as if *everything* in Matthew had to be tinted to Jewishness (or, for that matter, squash any gospel into always parroting a party line of our own making). For instance, even though virtually everyone agrees that Matthew is written to Jews and Luke to Gentiles, notice the two illustrations charted below that are precisely the opposite of a force fit.

MATTHEW— Jewish Gospel	LUKE— Gentile Gospel
Mt. 2:1-12 Gentile Wise Men visit the Christ Child.	Lk. 2:25-38 Two elderly Jewish people identify the baby in the Temple.
Mt. 8:5-13 Concerning the non-Jewish centurion only Matthew inserts 8:11, 12.	Lk. 7:1-10 Only Luke mentions that the "elders of the Jews" (7:3) endorse the non-Jew by saying that he "loves our nation and has built our synagogue" (7:5).

In ancient Greek mythology, Procrustes was the ogre who ran the ancient motel where he cut off people's feet who were too tall for his bed or stretched the short ones to fit. Hence, let's not be procrustean about expecting the Gospels to act like our puppets—doing what we have dictated that they shall do.

Having shot up that red flare of warning, let's go on to see how Matthew targets the Jews in this gospel. If we possessed only a certain set of verses in Matthew, we might say that he was so pro-Jewish as to be prejudiced against Gentiles. For instance, Jesus is given His name in 1:21 "because he will save *his people* from their sins." This makes Him a Jesus for Jews.

Only in Matthew's Gospel do we find the material in 10:5, 6—"Do not go among the Gentiles or enter any town of the Samaritans. Go, rather to the lost sheep of Israel." The itinerary on that mission includes Israel alone.

Only Matthew—of the four Gospels—includes the Old Testament quotation of Hosea 6:6, and Matthew quotes it twice (Mt. 9:13; 12:7). I suspect that Hosea 6:6 had become Matthew's life verse. He understood what the pious Pharisees didn't understand—God announced, "I desire mercy, not sacrifice" (Hos. 6:6). Wait a minute! Who commanded the Old Testament sacrificial system in the first place? God—the God who also said: "I desire mercy, not sacrifice" (cp. Isa. 1:11-17).

Probably Matthew at his tax stand had been sneeringly reprimanded by some respectable Pharisee more than once: "Don't you know that you're being tainted by your contact with all these heathen Gentiles? You should be down at the Temple getting cleansed of your many sinful contacts by many sacrifices. You're ruining your testimony."

Nevertheless, Matthew met a Doctor who was not afraid of being contaminated by contact with the sinnerliest (Mt. 9:12). Just as no doctor can quarantine himself or herself away from the infected patient, so also the Soul Doctor (Jesus) electrified the goody-goodies by partying with a bunch of sinners (Mt. 9:10, 11).

 Is your church a hospital for sinners or a museum of "holiness"? Support your answer with some examples.

 National storyteller Garrison Keillor (former host of Saturday night's radio program *A Prairie Home Companion*) told a story that pinpointed the age-old dilemma of the Church. Clarence Bunsen (one of the regular characters from the fictional town of Lake Wobegon, Minnesota) and his wife had decided to take a Friday night to get away from the kids. Therefore, they took their boarded-over pickup truck out to use as a camper. Unwisely, they selected the local gravel pit to serve as their camper parking spot. (The gravel pit is where the local teenagers went to neck.)

Mrs. Bunsen decided to get out of there; meanwhile Clarence was in the back of the pickup getting undressed. The truck was not automatic, and Mrs. Bunsen had rarely driven it. Hence, she took off with a lurch—and ejected Clarence out the back end of the truck into the gravel pit, clothesless! It had turned rather cold, and Clarence could imagine the teenagers yukking it up at the sight they saw. He couldn't catch his wife in the truck, but managed to climb out of the gravel pit and head on foot for the nearest house.

The house was owned by two older sisters who lived alone. Clarence rang the doorbell; then he ducked behind a porch post. He could see the two sisters peering out from behind the curtains, discussing what to do about the unclothed Clarence.

That scene, said Keillor, epitomizes the ongoing dilemma of the Church—to risk reaching out to help people in questionable predicaments or to preserve it's reputation against possible contamination. Sanctimonious separatism is not Christ's kind of holiness. As David Augsburger entitled his book, *Witness Is Withness.*

 Holy Toledo! Have you ever heard people use that expression? What do Toledo, Ohio, and Matthew 1 have in common? More than you might expect. Probably Toledo, Ohio, is named for Toledo, Spain. Therefore, "Toledo" must be Spanish, right? Wrong. According to *National Geographic* Toledo, Spain, once contained a large colony of Jews.

Toledoth is a Hebrew word for "generations" ["account of" in NIV]. The entire Book of Genesis is structured around ten genealogies (with the formula, "these are the generations [*toledoth*] of." See Genesis 2:4, 5; 5:1; 6:9; 10:1; 11:10, 27; 25:12, 19; 36:1; and 37:2.). Consequently, when Matthew opens his gospel with "The book of the generation[s] of Jesus Christ (KJV)" it is virtually his way of proclaiming a new genesis, a brand new beginning taking place with Jesus.

In contrast to Luke's Gentilic Gospel (which goes all the way back to Adam in its family tree in chapter 3), Matthew goes back in his genealogy to the father of the Hebrew people, Abraham (Mt. 1:1, 2).

Matthew's Gospel is punctuated with an Old Testament formula of fulfillment, giving it a distinctively Jewish flavor. "All this took place to fulfill what the Lord had said through the prophet" (Mt. 1:22)—or some similar formula—is found numerous times. For examples, look up Matthew 1:22, 23; 2:5, 6; 2:15; 2:17, 18; 2:23; 4:14-16; 8:17; 12:17-21; 13:35; 21:4, 5; 26:31; 26:54; 26:56; and 27:9, 10. Thus, Matthew's Gospel is but the counterpart to the Jewish operations manual—the Old Testament. Ralph Martin claims that Matthew "quotes the Old Testament 41 times [and about] . . . half are found in no other New Testament book. And of the 41 texts, 37 carry the introductory formula 'that it might be fulfilled.' "[2] In a larger estimate Graham Scroggie asserts that all the allusions to and quotations from the Old Testament in Matthew are "about one hundred and thirty."[3]

Another expression found only in Matthew, which would seem to carry Jewish flavoring, is "the Kingdom of heaven" (found 33 times in the Authorized Version). It's companion phrase, "the kingdom of God," used in the other Gospels, is found only five times in Matthew. Often Jews tended to speak in a roundabout way about God (cf. Mt. 5:34). Hence, Matthew prefers "kingdom of heaven" to "kingdom of God."

Only in Matthew's Gospel do we find the exclusive sounding, "I was sent only to the lost sheep of Israel" (Mt. 15:24). Indeed, if this sort of verse were the only strand of teaching, a case could be made that Jesus was quite a racial bigot.

Jewish Titles of Messiah

The title "Son of David" is found eight times in Matthew (in contrast with three each in Mark and Luke). Such a title would have less meaning to Mark's Roman readers and Luke's Gentile readers. All that is embodied in this title is a preeminent fulfillment of II Samuel 7:12-17 (cf. Lk. 1:31-33). Actually the first use of the expression so far available comes from the middle of the first century B.C. The apocryphal Psalms of Solomon prayed, "Raise up unto them their king, the son of David . . . that he may reign over . . . Israel" (Ps. Sol. 17:23). Matthew's Gospel then opens on the trumpet note sounded to "the son of David" (Mt. 1:1).

Another title appropriately treated here (although it is in no way exclusive or distinctive to Matthew) is "Messiah." In the Authorized Version it is found twice and in the New Testament only in John's Gospel (1:41; 4:25). In both those verses it is implied that *Messiah* is the Hebrew equivalent to the Greek word *Christ*. Both words mean "anointed" and refer to God's selected deliverer.

Often Protestants labor under a great misconception due to preaching they have heard. Some preachers used the title Messiah so frequently that listeners might gather the impression that the term was sprinkled throughout the Old Testament, but the title "the Messiah" does not occur in the Authorized Version of the Old Testament (except for Dan. 9:25, 26). The term "anointed" (equivalent to Messiah) does occur in classic passages like Psalm 2:2.

Another misconception that many Protestants frequently labor under is that Jews had a monolithic, clear-cut party line about what their Messiah would be like. However, even in the New Testament pages there are varying views. For instance,

1. In some cases "the Prophet" (of Deut. 18:15, 18) was viewed as someone different from "the Christ" (or Messiah). See John 1:20-25 where "the Prophet" and "the Christ" are obviously considered to be different by certain "priests and Levites" (1:19). Similarly, in John 7:40-42 some Jews call Jesus "the Prophet" while "others said, 'He is the Christ,' " showing that they conceived of these two as altogether different characters.

2. Jewish groups disagree about Messiah's manifestation (compare Jn. 7:26, 27 with 7:41, 42). Passages such as these demonstrate that during Jesus' time there was no all-embracing "Messiah theology."

These varying viewpoints on Messiah appear even more pronounced when one surveys non-Biblical Jewish literature, particularly between the Old and New Testaments. Below are some examples:

- The Jewish Psalms of Solomon (ch. 17)—from the first century before Christ—announced:

    And he shall be a righteous king . . . over them,
        And there shall be no unrighteousness in his days . . .,
    For all shall be holy, and
            their king the anointed [Messiah] of the Lord.
        —quoted from William Barclay, *Jesus As They Saw Him,*

- The Book of Enoch (48:10)—about the first century B.C.—condemned those who "denied the Lord of Spirits and his Anointed" (cp. Lk. 2:11, 26, and Acts 4:26).
- In a vision with an eagle and a lion sounding like and springing from those in Daniel, II Esdras 12:31 interpreted (about A.D. 150-250): "And as for the lion whom you saw . . . this is the Messiah."
- The Jewish monastic-type community at Qumran, inhabited most likely by a group called Essenes, held to two Messiahs—a priestly Messiah and a kingly Messiah.
- Perhaps the best intertestamental passage to show how varying Jewish views on Messiah could be is II Esdras 7:28, 29:

> For my son the Messiah shall be
> revealed . . . and those who remain
> shall rejoice four hundred years
> [contrast Rev. 20:6]. And after
> these years my son the Messiah shall
> die, and all who draw human breath.

This last quoted excerpt shows how fluid were the Jewish views floating around when Jesus was first called the Messiah (or Christ; Acts 2:36; 9:22; 17:3).

To the pagan Pilate's mind, the term "Christ" had to be explained as "a king" (Lk. 23:2). Consequently, he asked Jesus, "Are you the king of the Jews?" (Lk. 23:3). This, then, is the royal figure that Gentile magi came to Judea to find—the "king of the Jews" (Mt. 2:2).

Beyond Jewishness

Matthew is the most Jewish of all the gospels. It was written by a Jew for Jews. While this is true, it is precisely at this seam that Matthew shows us how Jesus' new wine bursts the time-worn wineskins.

Matthew was the Jew (who in his Jewishness as a tax man) was ever at odds with his Jewishness. Matthew's is a Gospel that supercedes mere Jewishness. As R. G. Lee once said, "If our hearts are not 25,000 miles in circumference, they are too small."[4] Jesus' new wineskin must be world inclusive.

To those smug and snug in their religious racialism Jesus said (only in Matthew), "I tell you the truth, I have not found [as in the Roman centurion at Capernaum] anyone in Israel with such great faith. I say to you that many [i.e., Gentiles] will come from the east and the west, and will take their places at the [Messianic] feast with Abraham, Isaac and Jacob in the kingdom of heaven. But [those who wrongly suppose they are automatically] the subjects of the kingdom will be thrown outside" (Mt. 8:10-12).

Only in Matthew's Jewish-tinted Gospel is the accusation of Jesus recorded: "I tell you that the kingdom of God will be taken away from you and given to a people [i.e., the Gentiles] who will produce its fruit" (Mt. 21:43). This is one of those rare spots where Matthew abandons his favorite expression "kingdom of heaven" for "kingdom of God."

Matthew's Gospel moves up to its pinnacle in the classic statement of the Great Commission in Matthew 28:18-20.

The most Jewish of gospels closes with the command to "make disciples of all nations." One might even render it: "make disciples of the Gentiles." Thus, the tax collector who once worked to make money for his Gentile overlords now had become a debtor in spiritual currency to them.

Notice the all-comprehensiveness of Matthew's commission. "*All* authority" is claimed by Christ (vs. 18) to make disciples of "*all* nations" (vs. 19) to teach the disciples to obey "*everything*" Christ commanded (vs. 20). And Christ's presence is guaranteed "*always*, to the very end of the age" (vs. 20).

> All authority.
> All places.
> All commands.
> All time.

It is a gospel of all-ness. Believers must be big minded, not bigots.

Just as God informed Jacob, "I am with you . . . wherever you go" (Gen. 28:15), so Christ informs His apprentices, "I will be with you always." After all, He is the Immanuel ("God with us") of Matthew 1:25.

Like children riding atop C. S. Lewis's Narnia lion, Aslan, Christians can bank upon this Gibraltar promise of Jesus. With his left arm hanging limp at his side (crushed by a lion), the gaunt and haggard missionary-explorer David Livingstone stood before the University of Glasgow in Scotland, where they were to confer upon him the Doctor of Law degree. "Would you like me to tell you what supported me through all the years of exile among people whose language I could not understand, and whose attitude towards me was always uncertain and often hostile? It was this: 'Lo, I am with you alway[s], even unto the end of the world' [Mt. 28:20]. On those words I staked everything, and they never failed! It is the word of a gentleman of the most strict and sacred honour, so there's an end of it!"[5] Yes, those words are the words

of a global Gentleman of the most strict and sacred honor—and that
puts an end to it.

> There's a wideness in God's mercy,
>   Like the wideness of the sea;
> There's a kindness in His justice
>   Which is more than liberty.
>
> But we make His love too narrow
>   By false limits of our own,
> And we magnify its strictness
>   With a zeal God will not own.
>   —Frederick Faber

CHAPTER

4

JESUS AS NEW MOSES
Matthew's Messiah

The critic Renan claimed Matthew's Gospel was the most important book ever written. William Barclay called it "the most important single document of the Christian faith, for in it we have the fullest and the most systematic account of the life and the teaching of Jesus."[1] Lorman Petersen concurred by calling it "the most complete record of the life, works and words of Jesus Christ in existence."[2]

One reason it is so important is that Matthew has over 300 verses found nowhere else in the Gospels, including much of the Sermon on the Mount in Matthew 5—7.

Although the following statement will need to be modified somewhat, we can say that Matthew gives us five sections of Jesus' lengthy teaching. (Repeat the sentence you memorized on Matthew.) These five blocs are charted below.

CHAPTERS	CLOSING FORMULA
5—7	"When Jesus had finished saying these things" (7:28)
10	"After Jesus had finished instructing his twelve disciples" (11:1)
13	"When Jesus had finished these parables" (13:53)
18	"When Jesus had finished saying these things" (19:1)
24, 25	"When Jesus had finished saying all these things" (26:1)

To Jewish thinking the number five might trigger upon the mind screen the five sacred books of the Torah, or Pentateuch (Genesis—Deuteronomy). This might be a way of implying to a Jew: your new Moses is here! Matthew supplies the new Torah.

The reason we stated above that this fivefold scheme might need modifying is that though chapter 23 does contain a lengthy speech of Jesus—in denouncing the Pharisees and scribes—it does not end with the same sort of verbal formula that the other extended teachings do.

Words and Works

Matthew appears to follow an alternating arrangement of Jesus' words and works (as does the Gospel of John). About three-fifths of Matthew's Gospel consists of the words of Jesus. Note the alternating arrangement of chapters below.

Works (1—4)
    Words (5—7)
Works (8, 9)
    Words (10)
Works (11, 12)
    Words (13)
Works (14—17)
    Words (18)
Works (19—22)
    Words (23—25)
Works (26—28)

MATTHEW OUTLINED

Here is a sketchy outline of Matthew:

I. *The King's Coming (1:1—4:11)*

This includes both His incoming to our planet and into the interest of the public.

A. His Ancestry (chap. 1). To be "King of the Jews" (2:2), Jesus must be "the son of David" (1:1; cf. II Sam. 7:16; Isa. 9:7; Jer. 23:5; 30:9; 33:17; Ezek. 34:23, 24; 37:24; Hos. 3:5; Lk. 1:32; Rev. 22:16).

Matthew arranges his genealogy (1:1-17) in three sets of arbitrarily chosen groups of 14 names (1:17). Three 14's would equal six 7's, making Jesus the seventh 7, or pinnacle of perfection—according to numerical symbolism. Not only that, but David is mentioned twice in the genealogy (1:6, 17). In Hebrew the consonants have numerical equivalents: D = 4; V = 6; D = 4. Therefore, "David" totals 14. All this seems more than accidental for a man who dealt daily in numbers.

B. His Advent (chap. 2). Non-Jews arrive asking, "Where is the one who has been born king of the Jews?" (Mt. 2:2). While non-Jewish Wise Men were willing to travel perhaps hundreds of miles to find the King of the Jews, the Jewish professional scribes, who could pinpoint chapter and verse on Messiah's birthplace (Mic. 5:2 in Mt. 2:6), were unwilling to walk the five miles from Jerusalem (2:1) to Bethlehem to check out this astounding question of the Magi.

 What does the preceding paragraph teach us about the difference between knowing and applying the Bible? Can you give a modern illustration of the Wise Men and scribes?

YOU CAN'T TELL YOUR HEROD WITHOUT A SCORECARD

Herod the Great	Only in Matthew 2 and Luke 1:5; built Herod's temple; killed many of his own sons; a half-Jew;

When Herod the Great died in 4 B.C., his territorial pie was sliced three ways between his sons:

Archelaus (Mt. 2:21)	Got Judea, Samaria and Idumea till replaced by Roman governors in A.D. 6
Herod Antipas (Mt. 14:1-12)	Got Galilee and Perea (Lk. 3:1) and beheaded John the Baptist
Herod Philip (Lk. 3:1)	Best of the bunch; got Iturea and Traconitis

C. His Ambassador (chap. 3). We meet John the Baptist (presumably a priest, being Zechariah's son; Lk. 1:5) not in the Temple but "in the Desert of Judea" (Mt. 3:1). Just as Israel wandered in the wilderness before entering the Promised Land, even so God was getting a new Israel ready in the wilderness—by John's baptism—to enter into God's fullness.

It is generally held that to enter Judaism a non-Jewish

proselyte must undergo (1) circumcision, (2) baptism, and (3) sacrifice. Hence, by baptizing *Jews* (no less!) John was treating them as non-Jews. Their physical Jewishness was not enough.

D. His Assault (4:1-11). After the baptismal endorsement ("This is my Son," 3:17) came the Devil's assault ("If you are the Son of God . . ." 4:3, 6). Messiah must show His mettle in the face of temptation.

II. *The King's Growing Career (4:12—11:1)*

A. His First Mission in Galilee (4:12-25). The ominous—indeed omenous—news of His forerunner ("When Jesus heard that John had been put in prison," 4:12) meant that Jesus "returned to Galilee" (4:12). Appropriately this northern territory is called by Isaiah (9:1, 2) "Galilee of the Gentiles" (4:15). Jesus called four disciples "beside the Sea of Galilee" (4:18). On His first public teaching tour "Jesus went throughout Galilee, teaching in their synagogues, preaching the good news of the kingdom, and healing" (4:23).

B. The Sermon on the Mount (5—7).With all manner of splendiferous fireworks (Ex. 19:16-19), Moses taught Israel her constitution—the Law from Mount Sinai. Jesus, the new Moses, now uttered His commandments and constitution for His new Israel (Gal. 6:16; I Pet. 2:5).

Just as Moses' Law was divided into five units that we call the Pentateuch, so Matthew introduces five blocks of Jesus' systematic teaching. (Repeat your capsule sentence.) These five are:

Ethical: the Sermon on the Mount (5—7)
Evangelistic: commissioning disciples for preaching (10)
Enigmatic: the mysteries of the kingdom (13)
Ecclesiastical: sin and forgiveness in the coming Church (18)
Eschatological: the Olivet Discourse (24, 25)

To gain maximum benefit, read the verses designated by each section in the outline of the Sermon on the Mount.

1. Characteristics of Kingdom citizens (5:1-16)
   a. What they *are* as individuals (5:1-12). This section, called the Beatitudes, contains nine "are" statements. Those who realize their spiritual bankruptcy (5:3) "mourn" their sin (5:4). They are, as we say, getting

their act together—and so are "meek" (5:5). ("Meekness" is not weakness, but, as Barclay defines it, harnessed strength.) Consequently they have a magnificent obsession—to "hunger and thirst for *righteousness*" (5:6; note this last key word).

Having faced ourselves (5:3-6), we can face others—with compassion (5:7), purity (5:8), peacemaking skills (5:9), and an expectancy of persecution (5:10-12). Note that verses 3-8 are sandwiched together by the repeated phrase "for theirs is the kingdom of heaven."

  b. What they *do* with their influence (5:13-16). Kingdom citizens are to serve as having the: influence of salt (5:13), eminence of a hillcrest city (5:14), radiance of light (5:15, 16).

2. Contrasts for Kingdom citizens (5:17-48). Kingdom citizens are expanded in all dimensions. Their "righteousness" (5:20) is to be:

  a. Wider in its effect beyond external traditions (5:17-20). Probably the key verse in the Sermon is 5:20—"unless your righteousness surpasses that of the Pharisees . . . you will certainly not enter the kingdom of heaven." The Pharisees' "righteousness" revolved around "the tradition of the elders" (15:2).

  b. Deeper in its essence to internal attitudes (5:21-32). Note in 5:21-48 the six sets of contrasts, marked by "You have heard that it was said . . . but I tell you" (5:21, 22; 27, 28) or "it has been said [or "was said"] . . . but I tell you" (5:31, 32; 33, 34; 38, 39; 43, 44). In every case Jesus burrowed beneath the surface to the underlying attitudes.

  c. Broader in its extension to outer expressions (5:33-42).

 Are we to take Matthew 5:38-42 literally? If so, how and when should it be applied?

  d. Higher in its elevation to unprejudiced love (5:43-48). Just as God is perfectly fair with His rain and sun (5:45), we should be "perfect," i.e., perfectly fair (5:48) regarding all people (5:46, 47).

3. Comparison of Kingdom Citizens with Pharisees (6:1—

7:12). In five major areas Jesus compares "your righteousness" with that of that "of the Pharisees" (5:20). To do so, he selects three typical *Pharisaic activities:*

a. Giving (6:1-4);
b. Praying (6:5-15);
c. Fasting (6:16-18).

Note the repeated refrain in each of the three activities: "do not . . . as [or "like"]the hypocrites" (6:2, 5, 16).

This is followed by a comparison with two *Pharisaic attitudes*—toward *things* (or covetousness—Luke 16:14 specifies that "the Pharisees . . . loved money"); and *people* (or censoriousness—7:1-12). The Pharisees' reversed attitude was to love things and use people. However, B. J. Thomas's song puts it properly—"Using things and loving people—that's the way it's got to be." Consequently, we are warned:

a. Don't be ambitious about luxuries (6:19-24); and
b. Don't be anxious about necessities (6:25-34).

 If you want God only, you may have all else besides.

—Meister Eckhart

Therefore, to be citizens of "the *kingdom* of heaven" (5:3) whose "*righteousness* surpasses that of the Pharisees" (5:20) we must seek God's "*kingdom* and his *righteousness*" 6:33). We must neither be covetous (6:19-24) nor censorious (7:1-12).

 Is it always wrong to criticize? (Check Mt. 7:1 in light of 7:5 ["then"], Luke 6:37; John 7:12; and I Cor. 2:15.)

Correct criticism not only first corrects oneself (7:1-6) but asks God in prayer for wisdom (7:7-12).

4. Challenge to Kingdom Citizens (7:13-29)
    a. As enterers (7:13, 14)
    b. As teachers (7:15-23)
    c. As learners (7:24-29)

In each case two types of things are contrasted. This Sermon left people thunderstruck, for Jesus "taught as one who had authority" (7:29), as a new Moses.

C. Jesus and Miracles (8, 9). In a topical treatment Matthew clustered together ten miracles:

PASSAGE	MIRACLE	POWER OVER
8:1-4	Healing of Leper	Defilement
8:5-13	Healing of Centurion's Servant	Space
8:14, 15	Peter's Mother-in-Law	Sickness
8:23-27	Stilling the Storm	Nature
8:28-34	Gadarene Demoniac	Demons
9:1-8	Paralytic	Paralysis and Sin
9:18-26	Jairus's Daughter	Death
9:20-22	Woman with Hemorrhage	Physical
9:27-31	Two Blind Men	Blindness
9:32-35	Dumb Demoniac	Compounded Problems

Matthew 9:35—11:1 narrates Jesus' Second Mission through Galilee, but the omen of His forerunner's imprisonment (11:2-19) results in a two-pronged response:

> Woes on the Galilean cities (11:20-24), and
> An invitation to "come to me" (11:25-30).

III. *The King's Controversy with His Enemies (chaps. 12—16)*

Note below the alternating pattern of *Controversy* and *Withdrawal* in the chart below.

> Controversy with Pharisees (chap. 12)
> Concealment in Parables (chap. 13)
> Withdrawal by Jesus—upon John's Death (chap. 14)
> Controversy with Pharisees (15:1-20)
> Withdrawal to Phenicia; Canaanite Daughter Healed (15:21-28)
> Comeback to Galilee and More Miracles (15:29-38)
> Controversy with Pharisees and Sadducees (15:39—16:4)
> Withdrawal to Caesarea Philippi for Climactic Confession
> (16:5-20) and Revised Understanding (16:21-28)

Under this section of our outline (which covers Matthew 12—16), let's zero in on only one of the chapters: Matthew 13. It is a most significant chapter because it gives us so many of the parables.

KINGDOM PARABLES

In Matthew 13 there is a clustering of eight kingdom-related parables. Seven of these are prefaced by "the kingdom of heaven is like . . ." (vss. 24, 31, 44, 45, 47, 52).

THE PARABLE	ITS POINT
Sower and seed	Invariable variation in hearers' response
Wheat and weeds	Intermixture of good and bad till the end
Mustard seed	Insignificant beginning on to great end
Meal's leaven	Imperceptible, gradual growth
Hid treasure	Inestimable value
Valuable pearl	Inestimable value
Dragnet	Impurity inevitable till the end
House owner	Instructor in Kingdom has innovations

IV. *The King's Concern for His Disciples (chaps. 17—25)*
   A. At the Mount of Transfiguration (17:1-23). Following Peter's confession of who Jesus was (16:13-20) came the divine confession of who Jesus was at His transfiguration and its sequel (17:1-23). Both confessions are followed by Jesus' announcement of His coming death and resurrection (16:21; 17:22, 23). Jesus whittled away at falsely romanticized expectations His disciples still fostered.

 How can new Christians pick up overly romantic and blown-up ideas about what to expect the Christian life to be? In what ways have your expectations of Christian experience been chiseled down to reality?

   B. At Capernaum (17:24—18:35). Matthew the tax collector is the only one of the Gospels to include the miracle concerning the Temple tax (17:24-27). This is followed by one of Matthew's five blocks of teaching in chapter 18. (Repeat your capsule sentence that you memorized on Matthew.) The lesson from the little child (18:1-9) and Parable of the Lost Sheep (18:10-14)—both about "little ones" (18:6, 10, 14)—are followed by teaching about confronting sin (18:15-20) and forgiving sin (18:21-35).
   C. In Perea (19:1—20:16). Perea was on the east bank of the Jordan River. In this Kingdom Gospel more teaching is incorporated about "the kingdom of heaven" (19:12, 14, 23,

24). As always, Jesus was the Great Reverser. He reversed traditional Jewish teaching about divorce (19:1-12), children (19:13-15), how to gain eternal life (19:16-30). Indeed, 19:30 closes, "But many who are first will be last, and many who are last will be first." Next proceeds a parable on reversal, concluding with, "So the last will be first, and the first will be last" (20:16). Obviously, then, the parable in between (20:1-15) teaches that God's values are often the reverse of traditional religious thinking. Just as the rich young ruler of 19:16-30 expected to be rewarded for his lifetime production of goodness (19:20), even so the early-to-the-field vineyard workers in the parable expected their reward to be greater.

? How has God reversed one of your notions about a Bible principle or truth?

    D. In Judea (20:17-34). As "Jesus was going up to Jerusalem" (20:17) for the last trip, He announced for the third time His coming death and resurrection (20:18, 19; cf. 16:21; 17:22, 23). Jesus was still revising His Jewish disciples' mentality as he had to inform them that they were acting like non-Jewish rulers (20:25). In some ways they were just as blind as the two blind men whose eyes the Son of David healed (20:29-34).

    E. In Jerusalem (21:1—25:45). The generally held calendar of the events of Jesus' last week is charted below.

DAY	EVENT
Sunday	Triumphal Entry (Mt. 21:1-11, 14-17)
Monday	Cursing Fig Tree and Cleansing Temple (Mt. 21:12, 13, 18-22)
Tuesday	Controversy over Five Questions Plus Olivet Discourse (Mt. 21:23—25:46)
Wednesday	Silence
Thursday	Passover (Mt. 26:17-29)
Thursday evening to Friday morning	Gethsemane and Trials (Mt. 26:30-75)
Friday	Crucifixion (Mt. 27:1-60)
Saturday	Tomb Sealing (Mt. 27:62-66)
Sunday	Resurrection (Mt. 28)

45

"The Coming One" (Mt. 11:3, Berkeley Version) came to His Temple (Mal. 3:1; Mt. 21:12). The Jerusalem Temple had become a thieves' hideout for religious racketeers (Mt. 21:13). The cursing of the fig tree (Mt. 21:18-20) was a dramatic parable of the cleansing of the Temple (Mt. 21:12, 13). The fig tree was one symbol of Israel at the peak of prosperity (I Ki. 4:25; Mic. 4:4; Mt. 24:32). Since the Jewish fig tree had not produced fruit, it must be purged. A second symbol of Israel was the vine (see Isa. 5:1-7; Mt. 21:33ff.) Following the parable of the tenant farmers who killed the land owner's son (Mt. 21:33-42), Jesus said that "the kingdom of God will be taken away from you and given to a people who will produce its fruit" (Mt. 21:43).

PASSAGE	QUESTION POSED	PARTIES OPPOSED
Mt. 21:23-27	"By what authority are you doing these things [i.e., cleansing the temple]?"	Chief priests and elders
Mt. 22:15-22	"Is is right to pay taxes to Caesar or not?"	Pharisees and Herodians
Mt. 22:23-33	"Whose wife will she be of the seven . . .?"	Sadducees
Mt. 22:34-40	"Which is the greatest commandment in the Law?"	Expert in the law
	Jesus then asks the question:	
Mt. 22:41-45	"What do you think about the Christ? Whose son is he?"	Pharisees
Matthew 23—25	". . . from that day on no one dared to ask him any more questions" (Mt. 22:46).	

Matthew 23—25 includes two final lengthy speeches of Jesus—one to His enemies (Mt. 23) and one to His friends (Mt. 24, 25—the Olivet Discourse). Matthew 23 is a barrage of woes on the Pharisees and teachers of the law (23:13, 15, 16, 23, 25, 27, 29), ending with

"Blessed is he who comes in the name of the Lord" (23:39). Matthew 24, 25 deals with the Second Coming.

V. *The King's Crucifixion (chaps. 26, 27)*

The "King" of the sheep-and-goats judgment (of Matthew 25:31-46) became the tried and crucified King of the Jews (27:11, 37).

VI. *The King's Conquest and Commission (chap. 28)*

The crucified King of the Jews met His disciples "in Galilee [of the Gentiles; 4:15]" (28:7, 10) after His resurrection. Then He commanded in Galilee (28:16) with "*all* authority" (28:18) to "make disciples of *all* nations" (28:19) till "*all* the angels" (25:31) "will gather" (24:31) "*all* the nations" before Him (25:32) as King (25:34, 40).

5

PHYSICIAN AND PARABLE PRESERVER
Luke's Medical Language and Parables

As the Scot said rhymingly, "It's time to take a look (*luke*) at Luke." Here is a capsule sentence to memorize that will help you capture *some* of the distinctive flavoring of Luke's Gospel:

Memorize: **Luke is the beautiful literary gospel with unforgettable parables, emphasizing the poor, women, prayer, and the Spirit.**

This sentence in no way captures all that is unique to Luke, but it will give you a definite feel for a mix of ingredients contained in the Lucan recipe.

MEET DR. LUKE!

Folks who have been teethed on Bible facts and stories may be surprised to learn that Luke is called by his name only three times in the New Testament and is called a doctor only once. Luke never once mentions his own name in his writings nor does he provide any explicit bio-data on himself. In that sense he is quite self-effacing. He is named by Paul (his apparent traveling companion) in Colossians 4:14; Philemon 24; and II Timothy 4:11. His only identicard entry with "doctor" on it is Colossians 4:14.

It is generally assumed that Luke is a Gentile writing for Gentiles (in contrast to Matthew the Jew writing to Jews). This conclusion is drawn from Colossians 4:10-15. In Colossians 4:7-17 Paul names 11 acquaintances. In his listing of four names in Colossians 4:10, 11, Paul sandwiches these four relationships under the heading: "These are the *only Jews* among my fellow workers for the kingdom of God [with me at this time]" (Col 4:11). Therefore, most Bible students conclude that beginning in Colossians 4:12 and following Paul is naming Gentile co-workers.

This is why Bible students reach the conclusion that Luke is a Gentile physician. If so, Luke is the only known Gentile writer in the New Testament.

Paging Dr. Luke!

In 1882, W. K. Hobart published a classic called *The Medical Language of Luke*. Some modern scholars feel that Hobart overstated his case, for he claimed to uncover 400 terms in Luke's vocabulary that were tipoffs that Luke was a doctor. Nevertheless, a case can still be made to document the thesis that Dr. Luke does occasionally drop terms revealing a physician's background.

 What kind of personality traits and clues would you expect to find in an ideal doctor? What spiritual qualities do you have that are tailor-made for your current job or major role?

Just a few of these items would not be sufficient to build a case, but when we stack up all the evidence together, it does form a composite portrait of a genuinely observant, caring physician.

Dr. Luke was not one of the apostles, as were Matthew and John, so he did not see firsthand the incidents he reports. However, many feel that while Paul spent two years in prison at Caesarea in Palestine (see Acts 23:23—26:32, especially Acts 24:27), Luke was foraging about in Palestine and conducting personal interviews with eyewitnesses who experienced the happenings and healings during Jesus' ministry. For instance, how else would Luke have been able to report on items like Mary's private emotions (Lk. 2:19)?

Now let's rummage through some of the material where Luke (in comparison with the other Synoptic Gospels) puts his doctor's touch forward. By comparing the fever Peter's mother-in-law was cured of (in Mark 1:30 and Luke 4:38), we note that only Doctor Luke specifies that it was a "high" fever. That might not seem to us like particularly technical medical terminology (in our age of "cardiovascular," "thoracic viscera," etc.). However, in ancient medical terminology there were broad degrees of fever, and this would be like saying, "She had a stetson-sized, a Texas-sized fever."

By comparing the Gospel accounts we note that only Luke specifies that it was the "right" hand of the man healed in the synagogue (6:6 compared with Mk. 3:1). Similarly, Luke alone pinpoints the "right" ear of the high priest's servant as the object of healing in the arrest scene of Jesus (22:50, 51 compared with Mk. 14:47).

Perhaps the most amusing of these case studies is that of the healing of the woman with a chronic hemorrhage who touched the hem of Jesus' robe. It is initially amusing to begin with simply because of Jesus' question, "Who touched me?" (Lk. 8:45). That would be like being in a packed elevator or being jostled at a county fair and asking, "Who touched me?" However, the more humorous item comes as we compare Mark and Luke's accounts. In Mark 5:26 one almost gets the impression that she had suffered more from her doctors than from her physical suffering. Like the widow later who was robbed by the religious syndicate (Lk. 21:4), this woman "had spent all she had" (Mk. 5:26). By spending all her savings to get better, she only "grew worse" (Mk. 5:26). Reading between the lines, we almost get the impression that Mark laid some blame for her condition upon the medical profession. Enter Dr. Luke to the rescue! If we subscribe to the theory most Bible scholars accept—that Luke used Mark's earlier Gospel in the writing of his own—then we may ask if Luke is not correcting a misleading impression that he thinks a reader might get by reading Mark's account. Luke reports that "no one could heal her" (Lk. 8:43). There's no mention of physicians' fees! It is as if he is saying that the problem of the cure lay not with the noble physicians but in the woman's physical condition. In other words, don't knock the medical profession for not being miracle workers!

UNFORGETTABLE PARABLES

It's time to repeat your one-sentence summary of Luke. What is it?

 Dr. John A. Scott, professor of Greek at Northwestern University for 40 years, asserted that Luke "wrote the clearest and the best Greek written in that century." The first four verses (Luke's Prologue) are very similar in literary style to those of the great secular Greek historians, such as that of Thucydides (*thew-CID-ih-deez*). Luke has literary flair, especially as compared with the streamlined, get-on-with-it Greek style of the simpler Mark.

Luke was called by Renan "the most beautiful book in the world." Perhaps the most memorable ingredient in Luke's Gospel is his unforgettable treatment of parables. According to Graham Scroggie (*A Guide to the Gospels*, p. 351) 19 out of Luke's 35 total parables are only found in his Gospel. In other words, more than half of the parables Luke includes are not located elsewhere.

David Redding defined a parable by a comparative process of elimination: "What is a parable? A fable is a fantastic tale with trees and foxes speaking. A proverb is a [comparative] statement with no tale at all. An allegory is a story with each part robotlike standing for something. But a parable is a story, true to this house of earth, but with a window open to the sky" (*The Parables He Told*, p. vii).

Before examining several classic parables, let's consider six characteristics of parables. First, they involve comparison of earthly and heavenly. *This* is like *that.* Jesus' parables "became Jacob's ladder by which those from heaven come down to earth, and those from earth ascend to heaven."[1]

Second, they are clothed in lifelike color. The Good Samaritan parable could have been reported the preceding day in *The Jericho Herald Tribune*. Walter R. Bowie wrote captivatingly: "As a tiny child [Jesus] may have watched with fascinating eyes the bubbling of the leaven [Mt. 13:33] as his mother's fingers kneaded it into the meal. He had seen her mend the all too precious clothes which could so easily wear out [Mk. 2:21], and he knew that there came a time when no more new patches could be put on old cloth."[2] Could Mary have been the woman who lost the coin of Luke 15:8, 9?

Third, parables are curiosity rousers. Parables are the candy wrapper or intriguing book jacket that bids the imagination enter. It is as if a hearer is rafting down a river and suddenly caught by a swift current. The reader is suddenly swept in and pulled along.

Fourth, parables are conscience provokers. Dennis Schultz observed that a parable short-circuits "the cerebral screening process to get to the visceral" response (*Bible Newsletter*, October, 1984). Many of the parables close with a question for a clincher.

(1) "Which of the two did what his father wanted?" (Mt. 21:31).

(2) "Which of them will love him more?" (Lk. 7:42).

(3) "Which of these three . . . was a neighbor . . .?" (Lk. 10:36).

Howard Ham stated, "When one saw the point of any story [of Jesus], it was as if someone had taken him by the shoulders and turned him around bodily so that he looked at the world around him from a different stance."[3]

Fifth, parables serve as a covering to protect truth from the careless and calloused (Mt. 13:10-15). David Redding said parables *project* and *protect* truth. Matthew Henry wrote: "A parable, like the pillar of cloud and fire [in the Old Testament], turns a dark side toward the Egyptians, which confounds them, but a bright side toward the Israelites, which comforts them."[4]

Sixth, ordinarily a parable concentrates on only one point. Mark

12:1-12 is the only Gospels' parable that acts like an allegory. John 10:1-16 is similar, but the Greek word for "parable" in the King James Version of 10:6 is not the ordinary one. Hence, the NIV translates it "figure of speech." "The parable is like a lens, which gathers many of the sun's rays and brings them to focus upon a single point."[5]

Among the more famous parables found only in Luke's Gospel are those of the:

   (1) Good Samaritan (10:25-37);
   (2) Friend at midnight (11:5-8);
   (3) Rich fool (12:13-21);
   (4) Lost coin (15:8-10);
   (5) Prodigal son (15:11-32);
   (6) Unjust steward (16:1-13);
   (7) Unjust judge (18:1-8);
   (8) Pharisee and publican (18:9-14).

It is debated as to whether the story of the rich man and Lazarus in Luke 16:19-31 is a parable or not. In Luke 9:51—18:14 there are 349 verses distinctive to Luke, and by one count 17 of the parables only found in Luke are embedded in this midsection.

The remainder of this chapter will be devoted to an inspection of two sets of Luke's classic parables.

I. The Good Samaritan (Luke 10:25-37)

Good Samaritan—ha! There is no such thing as a *good* Samaritan! That would be the mind-set of many a Jew of Jesus' day. Such a notion is similar to the abominable racist one liner: "The only good Injun is a dead Injun." Jews and Samaritans had a long hate history in their past. Therefore, our all-too-eroded familiarity with the famous parable must be cast against this backdrop of racial hostility.

Those who are called "lawyers" or "scribes" in the King James Version were a composite of copyists, lawyers, professors, and theologians in the evolution of their job roles. They began historically by

   (1) *inscribing* or transcribing the sacred Scriptures in the pre-printing press era; therefore, they became the logical candidates for
   (2) *interpreting* legal cases (since the Old Testament provided the Jews with civil law) and for
   (3) *instructing* in the religious Mosaic Law; therefore, they were the equivalent of teachers and theologians ("expert[s] in the law," Lk. 10:25).

One of these Bible experts became the hairpin mechanism triggering Jesus' telling of the world-famous Parable of the Good Samaritan.

Clearly the theologian's motives were not aboveboard, for he "stood up to test Jesus" (10:25) and "wanted to justify himself" (10:29). Whereas the motive behind his question was questionable, the question itself could be said to be the world's most important one—"what must I do to inherit eternal life?" (10:25). The shot fired from the Bible expert's gun was answered by a double-barreled question from Jesus (10:26). (More than once Jesus answered a question by asking another question; e.g., Lk. 20:1-4, 21, 22). Jesus gave the Bible expert an A+ on the accuracy of his answer (10:28)—since he had cemented together Deuteronomy 6:5 and Leviticus 19:18.

 What answer would you have given someone asking the question in Luke 10:25? If your answer is different from the one Jesus approved in 10:27, why do you think Jesus said, "Do this and you will live" (10:28)?

 Donald Grey Barnhouse used the following illustration to illuminate his understanding of Luke 10:27—"Suppose you have been torpedoed in the . . . Atlantic Ocean. I come to you with an offer of rescue. You . . . say to me, 'What must I do to reach land?' 'Well, . . . you have a thousand miles to go. Thou shalt swim with all thine heart, and with all thy soul, and with all thy strength, and with all thy mind. On the other hand, if you will only admit that you are totally bankrupt at that moment . . . I will be able to lay hold upon you [and rescue you].' "[6]

If the Bible expert had done perfectly what Jesus said, he would have been justified (cp. Rom. 2:13). (Notice here in 10:29 that Paul's traveling companion, Luke, uses one of Paul's favorite theological terms, "justified.") Instead, the theologian "wanted to justify himself" (10:29). Therefore, he asked the question, "who is my neighbor?" (10:29) that became the launching pad for the parable (10:30-36).

The road from Jerusalem to Jericho was called the Bloody Way. Since Jericho was a winter resort like Palm Springs, California, and since the Bloody Way was honeycombed with natural cave hideouts, it was to robbers what the backwoods Colorado stream is to people fishing for trout.

We are not told which way the priest was headed, but if he was going to Jerusalem, it is possible that he may have been going there to fulfill his once-in-a-lifetime opportunity—to do what Zechariah the priest did in Luke 1:8-23. It is estimated that there were 18,000-20,000 priests during those times. They were divided into twenty-four platoons or groupings (see I Chron. 24:7-18; Lk. 1:5). Divide 24 into

18,000 priests and you can see that special sanctuary privileges were a rarity! If it is true that the priest in Luke 10:31 was headed to perform his once-permitted sanctuary duties in Jerusalem, then it is not surprising that he wouldn't want to risk defilement by possibly touching a dead man.

 What kind of excuses do you suppose the priest and Levite gave? Can you give a recent example of the same thing?

When Jesus' hearers fist heard the word "Samaritan," they may have thought, "Aha! Here's the villain returning to the scene of the crime." Alas, the bad guy turns out to be the good guy.[7]

There is an intriguing observation that may perhaps be made here. In Greek the words "bound up," "wounds," "pouring in," and "inn" are all found *only* here in all of the New Testament. It would almost seem that this sort of care is so rare that the vocabulary itself is a giveaway clue to its rarity! Amazing, isn't it—that risking love is almost as rare as a museum piece. How many of us would have pledged an open-ended expense account (10:35) for the rescue victim at the J and J Wayside Motel?

The obvious answer to Jesus' question stuck in the law expert's throat. He did not reply, "The Samaritan" (10:37). The theologian who "wanted to justify himself" (10:29) walked away from the Justifier apparently unjustified, for he had not passed through the turnstile of humility.

II. God's Lost-and-Found Department (Lk. 15)

Like three chewable, crunchy kernels joined together inside a peanut shell, so the three classic parables of Luke 15 contain a common theme. Luke 15 is "God's Lost and Found Department."

 Can you say in a single sentence what is the truth taught by *all three* of these parables in the chapter?

In answer to that question we cannot say, 'God loves the repentant," for neither lost coins nor sheep can repent. Repentance is only found in one out of the three parables. Furthermore, we must resist the impulse to go beyond the data of the text and say something like, "God restores backsliding Christians." Such an interpretation takes one giant step beyond the transparent facts of the text.

 What catchword ties together the closing of Luke 14 and the opening of Luke 15?

The triune parables here are couched in the context of Luke 15:1, 2. In the cast of characters are two groups. "Pharisees" means "Separatists." They were upright-and-uptight spiritual separatists, who were worried about "their testimony." They held that contamination was contracted by contact with these "riffraff," these "card-carrying sinners." As far as Jesus was concerned, God's welcome mat was out for sinners. Donald Cole said, "The only truly godly life that was ever lived was immersed in a sea of people" (*Interest*, 1969).

Contrasting with the separatistic attitude toward sinners was the Savior's attitude toward them. That is what gives birth to these three parables—the lost sheep, the lost silver, and the lost son.

Lost sheep	1 of 100	animal
Lost silver	1 of 10	mineral
Lost son	1 of 2	human

Both the ascending percentages (from 1 to 50 per cent) and ascending values (from animate and inanimate objects to a person) contribute to the literary technique of moving toward a climax.

We may imagine the shepherd in the first parable tracking the truant sheep by the pieces of its wool left in the thornbushes. Jesus, the Good Shepherd of John 10, thus aligned Himself with the attitude of the God of the Old Testmaent, who had said, "I myself will tend my sheep . . . I will search for the lost and bring back the strays" (Ezek. 34:15, 16). As the shepherd of the story left the safer shelter of the fold to seek the stray, are we willing to abandon our comfortable confines to seek the lost (cp. Lk. 19:10)?

> The shepherd went out to search for the sheep,
> > And all through the night o'er the rocky steep
> He sought till he found him;
> > With love-chords he bound him.
> Oh, I was that one lost sheep!"

The second of the trilogy features a lost coin, possibly missing from the woman's bridal dowry worn on a string around her head. Observe the contrast:

> a man outdoors (15:3-7)
> > versus
> a woman indoors (15:8-10)[8]

The third parable is one of the most famous of all the parables of Jesus. It is the tale of a runaway who threw away all he had. Consequently, he moves from independence (15:12, 13) to indulgence (15:13) to impoverishment (15:14-16).

What factors might the prodigal have blamed for his "lousy luck"?

The runaway's story became: big money—bit city—big bust! Ironically, just when his finances ran out, the country's finances did, too ("there was a severe famine" 15:14).

 Down isn't so bad when it gets you lookin' up at life.

—B. J. Thomas

It was a blessing that he hit bottom. Because of that,
(1) he came to himself;
(2) he came to his senses; and eventually
(3) he came to his father.

"God is in the pigpen emptying business."[9]

Ω The KJV's "he came to himself" (Lk. 15:17) is the sort of Greek word that might suggest the reaction of a fainting person to smelling salts. It is the same Greek word used of Peter in Acts 12:11 when he woke up (out of sound sleep). We say of someone who had been in a coma, "she came to." A. T. Robertson suggests it is "as if he [the prodigal] had been as far from himself as he was from home."[10] In other words, a sinner is one who is away from his or her truest self as God intended it to be.

The Parable of the Prodigal Son might even more properly be called the Parable of the Prodigal Father. One of the dictionary meanings of "prodigal" is *extravagant*. Just as the son was extravagant, or lavish, in wasting his inherited property, so the father was lavish in his loving welcome.

Whence to me this *waste* of love?
Ask my Advocate above.
See the cause in Jesus' face
Now before the throne of grace.
—Charles Wesley

The whole body language of the dignified Oriental father in the parable ("he ran," 15:20, cp. Gen. 33:4) is good news for humanity. The father figure engulfing his pigpen-perfumed son in a bear hug is representative of God's attitude toward us wayward rebels who have gone A.W.O.L. from Him. And what a shindig the father throws for his returning runaway rebel. God is like that!

6

STOREHOUSE OF SPIRITUALITY

Spiritual Emphases in Luke

Let's hear that capsule sentence again that you are memorizing on Luke. What is it? As we noted in the capsule sentence, Luke emphasizes prayer and the Spirit. In this chapter we will enlarge upon some of Luke's spiritual emphases—namely the themes of the Temple, praise and poetry, the Spirit, and prayer.

The Temple

First, let's begin where Luke begins and concludes his gospel—in the Temple. The Jerusalem Temple has been called "the epicenter" of Luke's Gospel, as an earthquake has an epicenter. Sprinkled throughout the Gentile Luke's Gospel are certain spiritual details omitted from the other three Gospels. Therefore, Dr. Luke is also a soul doctor.

Luke 1 and 2 covers a chunk of material not found in the other gospels. These 132 verses unique to Luke, although written entirely in Greek, have an underlying Hebrew writing style (except Lk. 1:1-4). Therefore, William Sanday called the first two chapters "essentially the most archaic in the whole New Testament" (*The Life of Christ in Recent Research*, p. 166). An expert architect being driven through your city might point out to you houses built from 1900-1930 by means of their architectural style. Likewise, a scholar of Biblical languages recognizes behind Luke 1 and 2 a foreign writing style.

Why is this the case? Probably it is because Dr. Luke conducted extensive interviews with people like Jesus' mother. Furthermore, the poetic eruptions in these two chapters also bear the imprint of Hebrew poetry.

Before moving to our Temple theme, observe the alternating arrangement[1] charted below. It is based on the key Old Testament words "vision" and "prophecy" (e.g., Jer. 14:14; Dan. 9:24).

LUKE 1 AND 2

1:5-25	Vision of angel Gabriel in Temple (to Zechariah)
1:26-38	Vision of angel Gabriel to Mary
1:39-56	Prophecy of Elizabeth and Song of Mary
1:57-80	Birth of John and Prophecy of Zechariah
2:1-20	Birth of Jesus and Vision/Song of angels
2:21-40	Prophecy of Simeon and Anna in Temple
2:41-52	Young Jesus in Temple

Meanwhile, back to the beginning. The emotional maypole for any ancient Jew had to be the Jerusalem Temple. Thus, that is where we find the scene set in Luke 1:8-11. We meet Zechariah (whose name, significantly, means "the Lord [or Yahweh] remembers") doing what he had waited to do only once in his lifetime (among 18-20,000 priests of that time). The Lord remembered His people by announcing through the angel the birth of Jesus' forerunner, John the Baptizer.

Who will put their imprimatur upon Messiah the Lord and where? The perfect people to do so are the aged Simeon and Anna (Lk. 2:25-38)—those who hover around the Temple, like the psalmist who desired to be but a sparrow nesting around the Temple tops. Simeon was "moved by the Spirit . . . into the temple courts" (2:27). Anna virtually camped in the Temple precincts (2:37). Simeon "was waiting for the consolation of Israel" (2:25), and Anna was "looking forward [unlike many elderly who dote on the past] to the redemption of Jerusalem" (2:38).

 As the physical precincts of the temple symbolized Simeon and Anna's spirituality, what might serve as a concrete symbol of spirituality for you or someone you know? Explain how.

The first—and only—place we meet the preteen Jesus in Scripture is "in the temple courts" (Lk. 2:41-50, especially 2:46). The temple teachers were astounded at this precocious, almost-adolescent Jesus. Some twelve years earlier Jesus had formally been presented according to prescribed ritual in the Temple (Lk. 2:21-24).

While it is true that the Temple precincts become a beachhead of divine operations in Luke, contrastingly we meet the adult introducer of Jesus "in the desert" (Lk. 1:80; 3:2). Out in the Judean badlands (similar to the terrain of South Dakota) we read the blockbuster words, "the word of God came to John" (3:2). The Old Testament is pimentoed with expressions like "the Word of the Lord that came to Joel," etc. (Joel 1:1). Therefore, in all likelihood the sledgehammer effect of that power-packed phrase eluded you in Luke 3:2. For the first time in over 400 years, "the word of God" was erupting into history again through one of God's spokespersons!

In Luke 19:45 Jesus "entered the temple area" (presumably the outer section called the Court of the Gentiles) and drove out the religious racketeers. The Lord, whom they didn't seem to be seeking (!), came "to his temple" (Mal. 3:1). He ousted the profiteers and, as it were, recaptured the Temple zone.

Significantly, the last thread of this Temple theme is woven in as in *the very last verse of Luke* (24:53) we zoom in on the disciples of Jesus "continually at the temple, praising God."

Praise and Poetry

Notice also the next-to-the-last word above in Luke 24:53— "praising." Another traceable theme throughout Luke is that of praise and spiritual song. Along this line in Luke we find many praising God (1:46, 68; 2:13, 20, 28, 37; 5:25, 26; 7:16; 17:15; 18:43; 19:37).

Song is often the spillway of a believer's praise. Luke 1 and 2 is a great repository of Christian praise poetry. Thus Luke has been called the first great Christian hymnologist.

Luke 1 and 2 contains five masterpieces of praise poetry (not counting the Ave Maria of 1:38-41). They are:

(1) Elizabeth's song (1:42-45);
(2) Mary's Magnificat (1:46-55);
(3) The Benedictus (1:68-79);
(4) Gloria in Excelsis (2:14); and
(5) The Nunc Dimittis (2:29-32).

Scroggie wrote: "These are the last of the Hebrew Psalms, and the first of the Christian hymns."[2]

? What would you cite as an example of a great Christian hymn? Get hold of a hymnbook and point out why you think this hymn is great.

Mary's *Magnificat* illustrates the parallelism of Hebrew poetry. Hebrew poetry, though not rhymed, is channeled into couplets. Couplets are pairs of lines that run side by side like railroad tracks.

 Parallelism is emotion catching its breath.
—Herder in Geoffrey Bromiley, *Historical Theology*

59

Mary's *Magnificat* is also a mosaic of phrases hoisted out of Hannah's Song in I Samuel 2:1-10. Compare the phrases in the chart below.

MARY *Luke 1*	HANNAH *I Samuel 2*
46, 47	1
49	2
52	4, 9, 10
53	5, 7

Zechariah's *Benedictus* (Lk. 1:67-79) can be divided into two parts:
  (1) Jesus' job description (1:67-75);
  (2) John's job description (1:76-79).

Count the "to do" phrases in these two sections. The two characters are not left (unlike some employees) guessing what they are *to do*.

 Suppose someone asked you, "What do you plan to do with your life in the next ten years?" What would you answer—in no more than two sentences? (No fuzzy spiritual sounding, unmeasurable generalities, please.)

Concerning the *Gloria in Excelsis* of the angels in Luke 2:14, note an interesting feature in the order concerning John the Baptist and Jesus.

John's circumcision *(1:59)*	Angel's song *(2:14)*
followed by	precedes
Zechariah's praise *(1:67-79)*	Jesus' circumcision *(2:21)*

In the first case (John's coming), song erupts afterward. However, in the case of Jesus' coming, Heaven started the celebration early. The angels' anthem burst through the sound barrier almost as if to announce: Heaven can't wait!

Simeon had, so to speak, stood on spiritual sentinel duty for many years. With the coming of Christ, he could request permanent leave of absence. *Nunc dimittis* is the Latin equivalent for "you now dismiss" (Lk. 2:29). Simeon asked his Commander in chief ("Sovereign Lord") to be dismissed from duty.

Thus, Luke 1 and 2 is a rich latticework of Hebrew poetry rendered in the Greek langauge. Ephesians 5:19 represents song as the spillway pouring forth from the Spirit's filling. Consequently, it is logical that Luke's Gospel should also be one that stresses the Spirit of God.

The Holy Spirit

Obviously, since Luke 1 and 2 is material distinctive to Luke's Gospel, any place the Spirit of God is mentioned will be a reference found only in Luke. Seven of Luke's 17 references to the Spirit are in these first two chapters.

"Elizabeth became pregnant" (Lk. 1:24) and so did Mary—but with a distinct difference. Both birth givings were more than average (Lk. 1:7, 36), but only Mary's pregnancy was apart from the agency of a human male and the normal process of reproduction (Lk. 1:34, 35, cf. Mt. 1:23-25). The virgin's conception is not to be construed in a crude way as if the Holy Spirit were mating with Mary in the Greek mythical sense of gods cohabiting with human females. In some parallel sense, as the Shekinah glory cloud overshadowed the Old Testament Tabernacle in the wilderness, so also the Holy Spirit "overshadow"ed Mary, so that the Word (Jesus) took on human nature and (literally rendered) tabernacled among us (Jn. 1:14).

Poetry and prophecy merge in three cases as being spawned by the Spirit of God in Luke 1 and 2. Elizabeth (1:41), Zechariah (1:67), and Simeon (2:25-27)—three seniors—are mouthpieces for the Spirit's speech. Five references are made to the Holy Spirit in conjunction with these three individuals.

 If the birth narratives of Jesus (Lk. 1 and 2) give a highly significant role to four elderly individuals, what does this imply for our relationship to the elderly? If Spirit-spawned poetry is prominent in these chapters, what does this imply about a believer's relationship to the arts?

Both in His baptism and temptation (which are basically positioned back to back in all three Synoptic Gospels) the Spirit of God is involved.

> In Jesus' baptism He is approved;
> > in Jesus' temptation He is proved.
> At Jesus' baptism He is attested;
> > in Jesus' temptation He is tested.

 What do these two events teach us about ups and downs in a believer's experience? How does it help to know that Jesus was "full of the Holy Spirit" at the same time that He was "tempted by the devil" (Lk. 4:1, 2)?

Of the Synoptic Gospels, only Luke specifically closes the temptation scene by recording the parallel to its opening statement about the Spirit:

4:1— "Jesus, full of the Holy Spirit, returned from the Jordan."

4:14— "Jesus returned to Galilee in the power of the Spirit."

Just four verses later we encounter another reference to the Spirit (Lk. 4:18). The text for His inaugural sermon in His hometown synagogue is Isaiah 61:1, 2. As "the Holy Spirit descended on" Jesus at His baptism, so also Isaiah forecasted of the Servant, "the Spirit of the Lord is on me" (Isa. 61:1). Just as being "full of the Holy Spirit" (Lk. 4:1) did not prevent Him from being solicited to temptation, so also having the Spirit of the Lord upon Him (Lk. 4:18) did not prevent a public turnoff (Lk. 4:28) and an assassination attempt (Lk. 4:28, 29). The breeze of popularity (Lk. 4:22) shifted rapidly (Lk. 4:28) for the Spirit-filled Son!

Just as the polarities of Satan and the Spirit are found together in Jesus' temptation in Luke 4:1, so just after Jesus said, "I saw Satan fall like lightning," He was "full of joy through the Holy Spirit" (Lk. 10:18, 21). Study also Luke 11:13 and 12:12.

Prayer

On about seven occasions, Luke shows Jesus in times of prayer which are not mentioned in the other three gospels. Luke's Acts is also pimentoed with and saturated in prayer (e.g., Acts 1:14-24; 2:42; 4:31). Indeed, prayer is the birthing room of the Christian Church. Jude urges us to "pray in the Holy Spirit" (vs. 20). Likewise in Acts it was "after they prayed" that "they were all filled with the Holy Spirit" (4:31).

Perfumed incense is arising. Smell it? That's where Luke's Gospel takes off. "And when the time for the burning of incense came, all the assembled worshipers were praying outside" (Lk. 1:10). People are outside in the spirit of prayer, while a priest operates inside with the symbol of prayer—namely, incense (see Rev. 5:8).

While prayer is not a punch-clock affair, Anna had probably netted over 25,550 days (365 days X 70 years) of prayer. In other words, Anna was a prayer habitué, a devotee of the discipline, not just in it for prayer flair (just as Jesus was a regular at synagogue—"as was his custom," Lk. 4:16).

Luke is the only one of the four Gospels recording that the Spirit descended at Jesus' baptism "as he was praying" (Lk. 3:21). Thus, the

Spirit and prayer are linked at Jesus' Messianic coronation ceremony, at His identimarking as the Servant of the Lord (cp. Isa. 42:1 with Lk. 3:22), and at the outset of His public ministry. However, prayer was no showpiece for Him, for "Jesus often withdrew to lonely places and prayed" (Lk. 5:16). Prior to the formal selection of the twelve apostles, "Jesus went out to a mountainside to pray, and spent the night praying to God" (Lk. 6:12).

Just as at the scene of Jesus' baptism, so also at the scene of His transfiguration, Luke is the only one of the Synoptic Gospels to mention that it was "as he was praying" (Lk. 9:29) that Jesus underwent the transformation of *glow*-ry that exteriorized the splendorama of His inward being. This glowingness was offset all the more by the (probable) nighttime backdrop. (Note that the disciples "were very sleepy" and descended from the mountain "the next day" 9:32, 37.) Assuming that the transfiguration occurred at night, interestingly, Jesus prayed a number of recorded times at night (see Lk. 6:12; 22:39-46).

Some have observed that the *only* prayer prayed *after death* (from hell, Lk. 16:23) occurs in Luke (16:24, 27, 28)—and it was not answered in the affirmative. Some prayers are pointless.

Luke is the only gospel that includes the account of the penitent thief (Lk. 23:39-43). By contrast with the unanswered prayer out of hell (Lk. 16:24, 27, 28), the prayer of the condemned criminal is promised "paradise" within 24 hours (Lk. 23:43).

In the gospel of prayer, Luke's Gospel, the last words emitted by the crucified Christ are a prayer—a Jewish child's bedtime prayer (Ps. 31:5 in Lk. 23:46). Note the interlinking of "spirit" and prayer at Jesus' final breath.

The Emmaus Road experience is found only in the Gospel of Luke (24:13-35). Significantly, the risen Christ makes His identity known in prayer (Lk. 24:30, 31).

Luke alone narrates two parables on persistent praying. In a third parable only in Luke, Paul's friend records the attitude of one who is justified—and it is revealed in the context of prayer (Lk. 18:10-14).

TWO PARABLES ON
PERSISTENT PRAYER

Luke 11:5-8	*Luke 18:1-8*
persistent man seeking food	persistent widow seeking justice
from man asleep	from unjust judge
Because of persistence "he will . . . give to him" (11:8)	"they should always pray and not give up" (18:1)

Blaise Pascal once indicated that there are two types of people in the world: the righteous, who are convinced they are sinners and sinners, who are convinced they are righteous. There could hardly be a more clear-cut case of this than the Parable of the Pharisee and the Tax Collector (Lk. 18:9-14). In both cases prayer becomes the picture window of their souls. Moreover, we find ourselves back where we began this chapter—in the Temple precincts. One respectable, spiritually committed man wanted desperately to vindicate himself; another cried out, "God, have mercy on me, a sinner." The admission of spiritual bankruptcy is the key to admittance to the vaults of Heaven.

 What lesson do you learn from Jesus' protracted praying at both His baptism and choosing of the twelve apostles?

CHAPTER
7

FORGOTTEN FACES
Luke's Social Stress

Who could forget the lovable country doctor after having watched *Lassie, Come Home?* Or the ideal doctor (enshrined by Norman Rockwell) with his stethescope taking the heartbeat of a little girl's doll? Even the wry Doc Adams, one of the stock of characters on TV's *Gunsmoke,* was committed irretrievably to his duty of serving people. Many a doctor has entered hovel and mansion, treated famous and infamous.

As it were, by means of the clinical cases he gathered from interviewees who witnessed the Great Physician on duty, Dr. Luke has given us a dramatic portrayal of the spiritual and social ills Christ came to treat.

Some have called Luke the first Christian socialist. While those of other political persuasions might wish to debate that sataement, Luke does present a Christ who is concerned with all classes of society. Luke's Christ is at home with folks that the moral majority of that day felt ill at ease around. Luke provides pen portraits of neglected groups upon which even the other Gospels do not focus their lenses.

Before surveying this social spectrum of the "little people" in history, we must consider the fact that Luke is aware of the VIPs of his day. In fact, Luke notices these notables more than the other Gospels. For instance, only Luke (of the gospel writers—in 2:1, 2 and 3:1, 2) affords us precise dates by means of referring to the Roman emperors.

The social climate of ancient history was far less conducive to minorities, poverty, etc., than today. Yet in Luke's Gospel the spiritual must intersect the social if it is to stand in the spirit of Christ.

How would you feel if you were born a native American Indian and (in "America the Beautiful") you were expected to sing:

> O beautiful, for pilgrim feet,
>   Whose stern, impassioned stress
> A thoroughfare for freedom beat
>   Across the wilderness. ?

The Life of Lives in Luke's Gospel intersects all economic, ethnic, and environmental strata. In this chapter we will confront Christ's concern for the poor (and rich), women, Samaritans, and spiritual outcasts. Dr. Luke places his stethescope not merely upon people's physical plight, but raises our consciousness about deeper concerns.

The Poor

Perhaps the keynote to this first issue is struck when Messiah unrolls the sacred scroll of Scripture and reads the manifesto of His mission in His hometown synagogue:

> "The Spirit of the Lord is on me . . .
>   to preach good news to the poor" (Lk. 4:18).

As a baby, Jesus was not laid in some pretty baby crib. Gordon MacDonald proposed: "When automakers introduce new lines of cars, they select Detroit's Cobo Hall, Houston's Astrodome, or New York's Madison Square Garden for the event," but when He introduced His own Son to our planet, "God broke all the promotional rules" (*Eternity*, December, 1977). Martin Luther called the Christ child's cradle "the feedbox of a donkey." Jesus could empathize with the poor because He Himself became poor (II Cor. 8:9).

How must Jesus feel when Christians turn up their noses at the poor, or simply screen them out altogether?

When Mary and Joseph made the formal presentation of the child at the Temple according to prescribed religious regulations (Lev. 12:8), by the category of her offering she classified herself according to economic level—she was poor. Only in Luke's account do we find poor shepherds paying a visit to the manger-laid baby.

Compare one of the beatitudes from Matthew and Luke. What observation do you make about Luke's approach?

Matthew 5:3	Luke 6:20
"Blessed are the poor in spirit, for theirs is the kingdom of heaven."	"Blessed are you who are poor, for yours is the kingdom of God."

66

Luke does not spiritualize the beatitude ("poor in spirit") as Matthew does. For Luke poor is poor. The Jesus who came to "preach good news to the poor" (Lk. 4:18) blesses the poor (Lk. 6:20). Consequently, the Messianic job description stipulated by Isaiah 61:1, 2 was being executed.

? Have you ever known anyone who carried out Luke 14:13, 14 ("When you give a banquet, invite the poor, the crippled, the lame, the blind, and you will be blessed") literally? Why do you think people who talk so emphatically about a *literal* interpretation of the Bible neglect a verse like this?

One was black; the other was white. One had not finished the sixth grade; the other had a Ph.D. One was rooming on skid row in Los Angeles; the other lived in middle-class Pasadena. In some ways they were as different from night and day. Yet both were Christians. As they shared a meal, explored the depth of life's meaning, talked about how the Bible impinged on their lives, the more formally educated of the two confessed that it was one of the most memorable conversations of his lifetime.

In the Parable of the Great Banquet (Lk. 14:15-24) the owner ordered his servant to "bring in the poor" and handicapped.

? Have you ever shared experience with anyone having a handicap? If so, what did you learn? How would you want to be treated if you had a handicap?

Notice that economic levels are referred to throughout Luke 15 and 16:

- The father in the parable of the prodigal son was obviously well-off, for he even had "hired men" (not slaves) to pay (Lk. 15:17).
- The runaway son in the story had reached the epitomy of poverty (feeding pigs, Lk. 15:15, 16), and the pigpen became his incubator for serious spiritual reflection.
- Significantly, the phrase in Luke 16:1 used of the shrewd steward ("wasting his possessions") is the same in Greek as that used for the prodigal son who "squandered his wealth" (Lk. 15:13).
- A part of the application from the parable of the shrewd steward (Lk. 16:1-13) lies "in handling worldly wealth" and "true riches" (Lk. 16:11).

- Immediately after the parable about "God and Money" (Lk. 16:13), we are informed that "the Pharisees . . . loved money" (Lk. 16:14).
- Finally, Luke 15 and 16 concludes with the story of "a rich man" and "a beggar" (Lk. 16:19, 20). In the life to come their situations have undergone a great reversal.

The Rich

Notice that Luke's is not a kind of reverse snobbery. Sometimes middle-class people are not merely prejudiced against the poor, but also against the rich. However, Luke's Jesus also interacts with Pharisees who "loved money" (Lk. 16:14). Indeed, Luke's might be called the Gourmet Gospel! On no less than three occasions is Jesus shown by Luke as dining with Pharisees (7:36; 11:37; 14:1).

 How would you feel if you sat down on a plane next to the head of a New York city corporation? How would you react if you sat down on a plane next to a muscular 35-year-old woman with faded jeans, leather motorcycle jacket, and several tatoos on her arm?

Women

Luke mentions 13 women not found elsewhere in the gospels. First, scan the tabulation below of some individuals found only in Luke's Gospel

     (1) Elizabeth (1:5-7, 41-45);
     (2) Anna (2:36-38);
     (3) Widow of Nain (7:11-18);
     (4) Woman of the street (7:36-50);
     (5) Jesus' subsidizers (8:1-3);
     (6) Joanna and Susanna (8:3);
     (7) Mary and Martha's contrast (10:38-42);
     (8) Woman bent over for 18 years (13:11-13);
     (9) Woman who lost a coin in the parable (15:8-10);
    (10) Persistent widow in parable (18:1-8).

Some of the pressed ferns from Mary's memory have been unleashed by Luke to shed their fragrance in Luke 1 and 2. Others remain locked in the revenue chest of eternity (Lk. 2:19).

Luke 8:1-3 specifies some material otherwise unrecorded by the other Gospels, in which we are told of a group of women (three of them are named) who were part of Jesus' traveling party when He was sowing the kingdom seed (Lk. 8:4ff.) throughout the countryside.

? What objections might some respectable people—even today—raise against a group of men and women traveling together as a team (as in Luke 8:1-3)?

Luke 10:38-42 is the only place in the Bible where we find this particular reminiscence about Mary and Martha. From this story many a preacher or Sunday School teacher has portrayed Mary as the meek-and-mild, meditative-type of woman. However, Moody's radio pastor, Donald Cole remarked that this perspective may miss the mark altogether. Mary could easily be seen here as an "uppity" woman, for she was breaking a sexual stereotype. She was doing what men of that day did—"listening to what he [Jesus] said" (Lk. 10:39). Thus, a sexist would say that she was usurping a man's role, acting unfeminine, etc.

Samaritans and Gentiles

Luke's Gospel narrates three stories about Samaritan situations not found in the other three Gospels:
   (1) rejection by a Samaritan village (9:51-56);
   (2) the Good Samaritan (10:25-37);
   (3) the one thankful Samaritan (17:11-19).

In order to feel the brunt of these stories one must have a handle on the hate history between the Jews and Samaritans. In 722 B.C. the Northern Kingdom of Israel was taken into exile by Assyria. While Assyria deported many of Israel's leading lights, they also imported into Israel settlers from outside into Samaria (see II Ki. 17:24). The intermarriage of the importees and left-in-the-land Israelites produced the mongrel mixture of Samaritans considered impure by Jews both racially and religiously. See also Nehemiah 4:1, 2 and John 4:20.

Only one who has experienced the irrational brunt of racial hatred or entered the explosive environment of racial misunderstanding can fully value what Jesus did on this score. It must be remembered that Jesus encountered barbs from both sides, for he was both the object of name-calling by Jews ("a Samaritan," Jn. 8:48) and was rejected by Samaritans for His Jewish mission (Lk. 9:52, 53). Therefore, it is all the more remarkable that after the insulting incident of Luke 9 we encounter Luke 10:25-37—in which the story's hero is none other than a Samaritan.

? Can you name at least two outright and two subtle forms of racism?

To show how sizzling such situations were, one only has to read Luke 4:22-30 (the aftermath of His inaugural sermon in His hometown synagogue of Nazareth). Notice that Jesus' first recorded sermon was a sermon against racial prejudice. Why didn't Jesus keep quiet when His peers were all amazed "at the gracious words that came from his lips" (Lk. 4:22)? The illustrations that detonated their killer instincts involved His insinuations about Gentiles. Note the parallel below.

> "There were many . . . in Israel in Elijah's time,"
> but God worked somewhere else (Lk. 4:25).
> "There were many in Israel . . . in the time of Elisha,"
> but God worked somewhere else (Lk. 4:27).

And the somewhere else in both cases was among the Gentiles! Horrors!

Riffraff

The God of the riffraff—what a God is Luke's God! This is no antiseptic, smug and snug, upright and uptight God. This condescending God has come "to seek and to save what was lost" (Lk. 19:10). The condemnation of His contemporaries is His compliment—He is "a friend of tax collectors and 'sinners' " (Mt. 11:19).

 Some wish to live within the sound of church or chapel bell;
I want to run a rescue squad within a yard of hell.
—C. T. Studd

By the Pharisaic perspective, Jesus was contaminated. Luke 7:36-50 is a case in point. Jesus was an invitee to one of three meals he had with Separatists (the meaning of "Pharisees") in Luke's gourmet gospel. However, the *invited* guest attracted an *uninvited* guest (possibly they were eating outdoors in the quadrangle when approached)—"a woman who had lived a sinful life in that town" (Lk. 7:37). This (apparent) prostitute needed no red letter sewn on like Hester Prynne in Nathaniel Hawthorne's *The Scarlet Letter.* Her invisible "A" broadcasted her immorality. In fact, Simon the Separatist thought to himself that if Jesus were a true seer, He would *see* her sinfulness (Lk. 7:39).

David Augsburger wrote a book entitled *Witness Is Withness.* This captures the essence of Jesus' contact with this prostitute in Luke 7. Some Christians only offer a hit-and-run form of evangelism to non-Christians, wondering why they have no takers.

Twice in Luke's people-oriented gospel the author tells stories of tax collectors (18:10-14 and 19:1-10). William Barclay tells of the amusing incident of someone in the ancient world coming upon a statue engraved "to an honest tax collector." Ha! "Is there such a varmint?" was the sentiment. In fact, we note how regularly in the Gospels tax collectors are lumped together with "sinners" (e.g., Lk. 15:1). We would not have had three of the world's greatest parables (Lk. 15) if it had not been for Jesus loving these tax collectors.

Pharisees "looked down on everybody else" (Lk. 18:9), but one parabolic tax collector "would not even look up to heaven" (Lk. 18:13). The first type of person expected everyone to look up to him (Mt. 23:6, 7), but the second—due to his traitorous task of taxation—had trouble looking at anyone, or looking up at all.

? What can you learn for purposes of Christian compassion from people's body language? How does the body language of the two individuals in Luke 18:9-14 symbolize their feelings?

The tax collector of Luke 18 becomes a foregleam of the "chief tax collector" of Luke 19 (vs. 2). Once more Jesus' lack of prejudice at either end of the spectrum is apparent. William Hendriksen noticed: "The connection between the closing paragraph of chapter 18 and the opening of chapter 19 is almost unforgettable; for (a) both events took place in Jericho land, and (b) in the first instance a *poor* man [blind beggar] became a follower of Jesus; in the second, a *rich* man did."[1]

If life remains true to form, one suspects that Zacchaeus was brutally kidded and taunted ("you sawed-off shrimp," "you little runt") as a child. He was the little fellow outside with a big hurt inside. So he probably figured, "I'll get 'em back someday." And he did—he taxed them (literally!).

71

The Branded

Anton Chekhov's first sentence in his short story, "An Inadvertence" is: "Pyotr Petrovich Strizhin, the nephew of Madame Ivanov, the colonel's widow,—the man whose new galoshes were stolen last year,—came home from a christening party at two o' clock in the morning."

Imagine getting branded with the incidental item that your "new galoshes were stolen last year." Other people are identified as "the fellow with the ears that stick out" or "the woman who scurries like a mouse." Many times people make someone's handicap his or her identifying feature—"a man . . . whose right hand was shriveled" (Lk. 6:6). How does the Golden Rule apply in these cases?

The small man with the big hurt became the big tax collector. This is the only place in the New Testament where "chief" is pasted onto the front of the Greek word for "tax collector." Therefore, Alfred Plummer labeled Zacchaeus the "Commissioner of Taxes" at Jericho.[2] Zaccheaus was "contractor-in-chief of local custom-dues. Under a system then widely prevalent, these [dues] would be purchased by him *en bloc* [in a lump] and then leased to underlings."[3] Zaccheus then is a live illustration buttonhooking back to 18:24, 27—"How hard it is for the rich to enter the kingdom of God," but it "is possible with God."

Like the woman with the hemorrhage, Zaccheus wasn't going to let the crowd rob him of Jesus (Lk. 19:4). For those who are desperadoes to see Jesus, Jesus is intensely interested in seeing them (Lk. 19:5). Alfred Edersheim said that Jesus "uttered the self-spoken invitation in which the invited was the real Inviter, the guest the true Host."[4]

 Ong-gng-gng-ng (that's not a word, so don't blink your eyes!). Does that below-the-breath, tooth-grinding sound remind you of something you've heard from a whiny, grumbling child? It's intended to get at the onomatopoeic [ahn-uh-maht-uh-PEE-ick] Greek word in Luke 19:7 for "mutter." The root of it is pronounced eh-GAHNG-gooh-dzahn. (Does that sound like grumbling and mumbling, muttering and sputtering?) Interestingly, this compound, funny-sounding word is found only here and in Luke 15:2 in the New Testament.

Zacchaeus was spiritually poor, but financially rich. The altered Zacchaeus vowed: "I will give half my property" (Lk. 19:8, J. B. Phillips). Who knows? To fulfill that, did Zacchaeus have to sell his house and move down in the world? Yes, Zacchaeus had been converted—from a taker to a giver.

72

CHAPTER

8

SIGNS, SEASONS, SAYINGS

Outline Structures in John

The next three chapters will look at a series of selected themes found in John's Gospel. In this chapter we will survey three outline structures in John, or three approaches to outlining this gospel. Therefore, chapter 8 supplies you with three trips through John. First, here's your memory work:

Memorize: **In John's Gospel miraculous signs are intended to inspire belief in the Son for eternal life.**

SEVEN SIGNS

The structural girders holding up the framework of the Gospel of John might be said to be the seven signs found as pillars in its overall construction.

In the four Gospels there are four major Greek words used to describe miracles. Three of them are clustered together in Acts 2:22— "miracles, wonders and signs." The fourth is [in Greek] "works" (Jn. 7:21; 10:32). In the chart below the various emphases of the four Greek words are highlighted so as to present a composite picture of Jesus' miracles.

VOCABULARY	RAISES RESPONSE	HIGHLIGHTS
"miracles" (literally, "powers") [Gr. *dunameis*]	Wham!	The power or stupendous strength
"wonders" [Gr. *teras*]	Wow!	A portent or something spectacular
"signs" [Gr. *semeia*]	Why?	The purpose or significance
"works" [Gr. *erga*]	Work!	The productivity in which the supernatural is natural for Jesus!

The Gospel of John uses two of these terms—"signs" and "works." The standard word for miracles in the Synoptics, *dunameis* (from which we derive the English word "dynamite") does not appear in John's Gospel. In John what would be extraordinary for anyone else—to do miracles—appears quite ordinary (merely "works") for the extraordinary Jesus!

The hallmark of this gospel, however, is the author's selected set of miracles around which he structures His portrayal of Jesus. They are called "signs" by the author (cf. 2:11; 20:30, 31). These signs are intended to elicit and evoke (20:30, 31). However, the author was well aware that the aim of miracles might be aborted by the unbelieving observer (2:23, 24; 4:48; 6:30).

The cartoon above makes an important point—namely, that many misunderstand the meaning of miracles. They get wowed by the dazzlingness of the miracles, and so the miracles become ends in themselves. However, according to John, miracles are to be seen as "signs." While traveling along a major highway, a person does not proceed to unpack his suitcases at a sign. The road sign is a pointer beyond the sign onward to the sign's destination. Miracles have *significance*. John 20:30, 31 indicates that Jesus' miraculous signs were posted as pointers to His person—"these [miraculous signs] are written [down] that you may believe that Jesus is the Christ, the Son of God . . . ."

What are the seven miraculous signboards selected by John? Six of the seven are found only in John's Gospel. They are charted below.

PASSAGE	EVENT	EMPHASIS
2:1-11	Water to Wine	Power over Chemistry
4:46-54	Nobleman's Son Healed	Space and Time (Remote Control Healing)
5:1-15	Bethesda Pool Healing	Bodies
6:1-15	Feeding over Five Thousand	Matter
6:16-21	Walking on Water	Nature
9:1-12, 35-38	Healing Congenitally Blind	Tragedy
11:1-46	Raising Lazarus	Death

+ a SIGN beyond all signs = the resurrection of the Son of God

SEVEN SEASONS

Another structural clue to John's Gospel is his use of time, particularly Jewish red-letter days. The Fourth Gospel is organized much more around chronological events than the Synoptics. Look up John's references to a specific "hour" (1:39; 4:6, 52; 19:14). John portrays Jesus as operating by a great invisible time clock (2:4; 4:23; 7:30; 8:20; 12:23, 27; 13:1; 16:32; 17:1).

Another intriguing possibility is the structuring of John 1 and 2 as if it were a brand-new alternative to Genesis 1.

GENESIS 1	JOHN 1, 2
"In the beginning" (1:1)	"In the beginning" (1:1)
Day one	Day one—delegation interrogates John the Baptist
Day two	"The next day" (1:29) the Lamb of God
Day three	"The next day" (1:35) John's disciples seek Jesus
Day four	(Possibly another day if the "tenth hour" is 4 p.m.)
Day five	"The next day" (1:43) Nathanael finds Messiah
Day eight: a new week	"On the third day" (2:1) [from the last] new wine is made

Therefore, John seems to present a schedule of seven or eight days, following the heading "In the beginning." It would appear to be a deliberate play off of Genesis 1. In that case John presents a NEW CREATION—as it were, week two since original Creation, when God is inaugurating something so brand new in Jesus as to be on a par with the Creation of the world. Indeed, "through him all things were made" (1:3).

In the first section of this chapter the seven signs are John's own selection. In this section the seven seasons are arbitrarily selected. It is not claimed that these are the apostolic author's arrangement.

I. Passover 1 (Jn. 2:23)

Steven Barabas observed, "The Passover was the first in point of time of all the annual feasts [see Exod. 12], and historically and religiously it was the most important of all."[1] Passover commemorated the night when the Lord passed over houses, and Israelites with blood-sprinkled doorposts were spared the death of their firstborn sons. It came to epitomize their emancipation from Egyptian enslavement.

It was around John's first recorded Passover (2:13) that the adult Jesus ran the religious racketeers out of their stockyardlike atmosphere in the Temple precincts. Like the 1950's cowboy Lash LaRue wielding his bullwhip, Jesus assaulted the priestly profiteers' hub of operations. This is the Aslan Jesus. (Aslan is the lion of C. S. Lewis's Narnia trilogy.) This is the untepid, nonanemic, unmeek and unmild Jesus. Dorothy Sayers once claimed that too often Christians take the Lion of the tribe of Judah and pare down his claws so that He retains all the ferocity of a polite tea party guest.

? Is your Jesus concept broad enough to fit *all* the facts? What elements about Jesus do you think many people conveniently overlook?

II. Anonymous Feast (Jn. 5:1)

John 5:1 mentions an ambiguous "feast of the Jews." This would seem to be something other than a Passover since John deliberately mentions three Passovers by name. It was likely the Feast of Purim (March), though it could possibly have been the Feast of Trumpets (September).

III. Passover 2 (Jn. 6:4)

The miracle of the feeding of the 5000 plus is the one miracle of Jesus recorded by all four Gospels. Jesus' second recorded Passover during His public ministry followed that memorable miracle. The spring season was then in evidence in Mark's mention of "the green grass" (6:39). Mark seemed to see the scene as a giant flower bed—with all the multicolored robes arranged into "garden beds" (the literal rendering of "groups" in 6:39) against the backdrop of the verdant hillside (as the hymn says, "robed in the blooming garb of spring").

IV. Feast of Tabernacles (Jn. 7:2)

For background material read Leviticus 23:33-43; Numbers 29:12-40; and Nehemiah 8:13-18. *Tabernacles* in this context should not be confused with Israel's wilderness Tabernacle, a portable worship sanctuary. By contrast, these tabernacles, or booths, were like open-air lean-tos—outdoor shelters made of leafy branches.

Josephus, a Jewish historian contemporary with John, called the Feast of Tabernacles the most sacred and important feast of the Jews.

The Feast of Tabernacles had a dual purpose. It was a simulated reenactment of ancient Israel's experience during the wilderness wanderings. But it was also an autumn harvest festival, "the Feast of Ingathering at the end of the year" (Ex. 23:16). Thus, it was somewhat similar to Thanksgiving in North America.

The picnic-style festival, requiring temporary residence in outdoor booths, took place from the 15th through the 21st day of the seventh

Jewish month (roughly our October). On each of these seven days, a diminishing number of animals were sacrificed (see Num. 29:12-40). About 450 priests and the same number of Levites were required for the sacrificial worship services of this feast.

On the seventh day, water would be drawn with a golden pitcher by a priest from the Pool of Siloam. The priests and people then marched back in festive procession to the altar of burnt offering at the Temple. All the while, they waved palm branches, myrtle, and willows (Lev. 23:40). Some say that flute playing and dancing accompanied the procession.

A threefold trumpet blast announced the arrival of the group. Upon reaching the Temple altar, the water from the golden pitcher was poured into a silver funnel on the side of the altar of burnt offering. People and priests chanted the Hallel Psalms (113-118) antiphonally.

On this seventh day of the feast, the priests would march around the altar seven times—as if they were marching around the walls of Jericho. Some say that Isaiah 12:3 was sung: "With joy you will draw water from the wells of salvation." Certainly this would be a moment tailored to Jesus' cry—to come to Him and drink (Jn. 7:37). Or if Jesus cried aloud on the eighth day, He would, in effect, be a replacement for the water-pouring ceremony.

AGRICULTURAL CYCLE

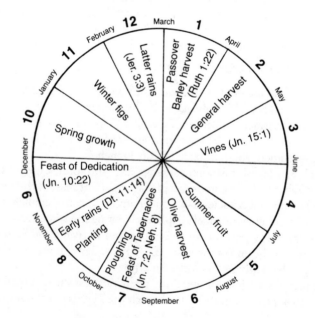

V. Feast of Dedication (Jn. 10:22)

This Jewish red-letter day came into being after the Old Testament had already closed. It dates from about 164 B.C. In 167 B.C. there arose what might well be the first campaign of religious persecution in history. Antiochus Epiphanes [an-TIE-uh-kuss ee-PIFF-uh-nees]—as it were, the Hitler before Hitler to the Jews—desecrated abominably the Jerusalem Temple altar of burnt offering. To circumcise male babies, keep the Sabbath, or own Scripture copies was a capital offense. Daily sacrifices were suspended, a sow was sacrificed, and sacred prostitution was instituted. This was certainly a miniature "abomination that causes desolation" (Mt. 24:15).

Three years to the day after the altar was desecrated (on December 25th) the altar was reconsecrated or dedicated. Thus, this 8-day feast is called "the dedication of the altar" (I Maccabees 4:59). Josephus, the Jewish historian, called it "the feast of lights," or Hanukkah.

The hero responsible for Hanukkah was Judas Maccabeus (his name means "the Hammer"). He was like the Jewish version of Zorro, a hero, and a genius at guerilla warfare. He recaptured and rededicated the Temple. For the Jews this was a declaration of religious independence.

VI. Passover 3 (Jn. 12:12, 20; 13:1)

At Jesus' last Passover it is possible that they were following the Roman arrangement of the triclinium (or three table arrangement). The disciples would have reclined on pillows on their left sides, leaning on their left elbows and eating with their right hands. Their bodies would have stretched out from the three tables at an oblique angle. The overhead sketch below gives an idea of how some of the disciples may have been arranged.

The reasoning behind the suggested positioning is as follows. Jesus must have occupied the position of Passover host. At one point John was close enough to lean his head back toward Jesus' chest to ask him a question (Jn. 13:25). "Peter motioned to" John to ask Jesus (Jn. 13:24). Jesus dipped the morsel of bread, called the sop, and handed it to Judas (Jn. 13:26), although He could have gotten up to do this. If Judas was next to Jesus, it would mean he was occupying one of the honored positions (Mt. 20:21) at the table.

VII. Now and Then (Jn. 4:23; 5:25, 28)

Bible scholars speak about *realized* and future *eschatology* (*es-kuh-TAHL-uh-jee*) "Eschatology" means a "study of last things." Popularly, this is often called *prophecy* (despite the fact that, in the Bible, prophecy covers both current insight by prophets—through preaching—as well as supernatural predictions of the future).

In the Gospel of John there is distinct reference to realized eschatology—where the future has already entered into the present (Jn. 4:23; cf. I Jn. 2:18—"this is the last hour . . . even now"). However, the fact that the divine future has impinged upon and irrupted into the present does not exhaust all the truth about eschatology. There are still panoramic things that are "yet to come" (Jn. 16:13). These two levels of eschatology can be witnessed in John 5.

REALIZED ESCHATOLOGY	FUTURISTIC ESCHATOLOGY
"a time . . . has now come when the [spiritually] dead will hear the voice of the Son of God and . . . will live" (Jn. 5:25)	"a time is coming when all who are in their graves will . . . come out . . . to live . . . and to be condemned" (Jn. 5:28, 29)
Spiritual resurrection	Future bodily resurrection

SEVEN SAYINGS

John's Gospel is famous for its 7 classic "I am" sayings. It should be noted, however, that these are the "I am's followed by a specific predicate (e.g., "I am the bread of life").

There are key references where the "I am" appears absolutely, i.e., without a predicate. For instance, to the Samaritan woman at the well Jesus made the staggering statement in 4:26, "He who is talking to you, I Am" (literally translated from Greek). The "I Am" here unquestionably flashes back to Exodus 3:14. Ethelbert Stauffer claimed that this title was "the most authentic, the most audacious, and the most profound affirmation of Jesus of who he was."[2] Similarly, Jesus audaciously asserted in John 8:58—"before Abraham was born, I am!"

Below we will survey the seven sterling "I am" sayings of Jesus:

I Am the Bread of Life (6:34)

Sigmund Freud, the father of psychotherapy, said, "The meager satisfaction that man can extract from reality leaves us starving." We are like John Newton, the hymn writer of "Amazing Grace" who had been left by an African slave trader in the care of his slave mistress, named "P.I." When Newton took extremely ill, P.I. turned on him. She tossed meager food scraps to him on the floor. Eventually he was forced to scrounge in the sand for tubers to survive, but that only made Newton sicker. What a parable of spiritually sick and starving humanity! But Jesus is the source, sustenance, and substance of life. All this is hinted at when Jesus says to us: "I am the bread of [your] life" (6:34).

I Am the Light of the World (8:12)

If we link John 8:12 with chapter 7, the occasion would still be the Feast of Tabernacles. Leon Morris observed that "the brilliant candelabra were lit only at the beginning of the Feast of Tabernacles." However, "there is also the fact that the candelabra were lit in the Court of the Women, the most frequented part of the temple, and the very place in which Jesus delivered His address."[3]

Before the time of Christ, the Greek philosopher Plato said: "We will wait for one, be he a god or an inspired man . . . to take away the darkness from our eyes." Jesus said, "I am the light of the world. Whoever follows me will never walk in darkness, but will have the light of life" (8:12).

I Am the Door (10:9, KJV)

 Your soul has a curious shape because it is a hollow made to fit a particular swelling in the infinite contours of the divine substance, or a key to unlock one of the doors in the house of many mansions.
—C. S. Lewis

Changing the imagery above somewhat, Jesus proclaimed: "I am the gate; whoever enters through me will be saved" (10:9).

> There was no other good enough
> To pay the price of sin;
> He only could unlock the gate
> Of heaven and let us in."
> —Cecil Alexander

I Am the Good Shepherd (10:11, 14)

Read Ezekiel 37:14-16.

 What else is there to make life tolerable? We stand on the shore of an ocean, crying to the night and the emptiness . . . . The world seems quite dreadful; the unhappiness of many people is very great, and I often wonder how they endure it.

> —Bertrand Russell, agnostic philosopher

> I, a stranger and afraid,
>   in a world I never made.
> —A. E. Housman, poet scholar

> We are his people, the sheep of his pasture.
> —Psalm 100:2

I Am the Resurrection and the Life (11:25)

In the celebrated musical by Kern and Hammerstein, *Show Boat,* the black deckhand sings the unforgettable "Ol' Man River." The lyrics pinpoint in a single line the gigantic dilemma of the human species: "Tired of livin', an' feared of dyin'." Similarly, a rock group of the early 1970s—named Marmolade—sang, "The world is a bad place, a terrible place to live in. Oh-h-h, but I don't want to die."

We have perfumed, mascaraed, and bouqueted the hideous specter of death in modern America, but the stalker continues his horrible, democratic rampage nonetheless. Meeting the stalker in a head-on confrontation at the grave of His friend Lazarus, Jesus insisted, "I am the resurrection and the life. He who believes in me will live, even though he dies" (11:25).

 Jim Elliot, martyred by the Auca Indians in the Amazon jungle, once wrote in his diary: "There's a sense of discouragement and doubt come over me . . . . There is a strong pull to the philosophy that 'chaos' created this lump of clay in his own image—and to let fall the whole gamut of theological arguments. Again, I'm held by the resurrection of Jesus Christ. Were it not that I believed that Jesus was seen of men and proved Himself to be supernatural in outwitting death, I would throw the whole system back to the troubled skies and take a raft down the Mississippi today."

I Am the Way and the Truth and the Life (14:6)

Richard of Chichester prayed "to know Jesus Christ more clearly, to love him more dearly, and to follow him more nearly."[4]

Christ is the way—
> without Him there's no going.

He is the truth—
> without Him there's no knowing.

He is the life—
> without Him there's no showing.

A taxi driver in Britain reported, "Only the other evening I picked up Bertrand Russell, and I said to him, 'Well, Lord Russell, what's it all about? And, do you know, he couldn't tell me'" (in the *London Times*). Perhaps John 14:6 comes as close to the "what's it all about" as anything. It announces Jesus as the Passport to God. He declared: "I am the way and the truth and the life. No one comes to the Father except through me" (14:6). Consequently, his followers could proclaim, "Salvation is found in no one else, for there is no other name under heaven given . . . by which we must be saved" (Acts 4:12).

I Am the True Vine (15:5)

It is not absolutely clear at what point Jesus and His disciples exited from the Upper Room. In John 14:31 Jesus said, "Come now; let us leave." In John 18:1 we read, "When he had finished praying [John 17], Jesus left with his disciples and crossed the Kidron Valley." If they had exited immediately following John 14:31, then they may have been winding their way through the darkened streets of Jerusalem past the Temple to cross eastward over that ravine called the Kidron Valley en route to the Garden of Gethsemane.

Jesus' allegorical teaching about the vine and branches may have been presented as they passed the Jerusalem Temple. There was a decoration over the Temple of Herod representing a huge golden vine. In a much earlier allegory Isaiah (5:1-7) had made the identification: "The vineyard of the Lord Almighty is . . . Israel" (5:7). Therefore, Jesus here became the ideal Israel. His people find their fullest fulfillment in union and communion with Him.

William Barrett stated, "Mankind may be only a tiny and meaningless freak within nature. We are homeless in the world." Not so, says Jesus to you. "I will not leave you as orphans," said Jesus (Jn. 14:18) just before He depicted a Christian's relationship as branches in a vine (15:1-5). In Christ I am, as B. J. Thomas's song put it, "home where I belong." The sense of belongingness for a human being finds its deepest rootedness in Christ the Vine. *Who I am* finds its fullest fulfillment in *Whose I am*, namely, in the I AM. I am of value because of who He is, the I AM.

CHAPTER

9

THE 3 R's

Leading Themes in John

Reading, 'Riting, and 'Rithmetic—those are the 3 R's of regular schooling. But what are the 3 R's of John's Gospel? What we are labeling the 3 R's (revelation, response, result) form the foundational theme flowing through the Gospel of John. These 3R's are:

(1) an external REVELATION (John's term is "sign");
(2) an internal RESPONSE (found in John's verb "believe"); and
(3) an eternal RESULT (namely "eternal life").

Notice how all of the 3 R's are found in the author's own explicit statement of purpose, John 20:30, 31.

"Sign"
1. External Revelation

"Believe"
2. Internal Response

"Have [eternal] life"
3. Eternal Result

EXTERNAL REVELATION

The first "R" has already been highlighted in the preceding chapter. "Sign" is John's code word for spotlighting seven selected miracles of Jesus. The NIV gets the force of this across by translating "miraculous signs" in 20:30, even though the term "miraculous" is not present in Greek.

Notice in the passages from John (quoted on the next page) how miraculous signs are a basis for belief (even if the belief is not the real McCoy in several instances).

84

2:11	"This, the first of his miraculous *signs*, Jesus performed . . .	and his disciples *put their faith in him*."
2:23	"At the Passover . . . many people saw the miraculous *signs* he was doing	and *believed* in his name."
4:48	"Unless you . . . see miraculous *signs* . . .	you will never *believe*."
6:30	"What miraculous *sign* then will you give	that we may . . . *believe* [in] you?"
7:31	"Will he do more miraculous *signs* . . . ?"	"Many in the crowd put their *faith* in him."
12:37	"Even after Jesus had done all these miraculous *signs* . . .	they still would not *believe* in him."

These miracles were meant to evoke faith in the person of Jesus. They were intended to function as signboards or highway signs pointing onward to Jesus as their destination. John wrote "so that you may believe" (11:15).

INTERNAL RESPONSE

The Gospel of John never uses the Greek noun "faith." Instead, consistently John prefers the active verb "believe" close to 100 times. The verb "believe" can be used in a lesser and greater sense. Evidently in John 2:23 it does not carry the full sense of saving faith, for Jesus did not believe in the Passover crowd (2:24) despite the fact that they "believed in his name" (2:23). Similarly, James reported a nonsaving belief on the part of demons (2:19) who both have an intellectual (they "believe that there is one God") and an emotional (they "shudder") response to the revelation of God they possess. However, a commitment of will is lacking. It is interesting in John 2:24 ("Jesus would not *entrust* himself to them") that the NIV's "entrust" is just another form of the same Greek verb rendered "believed" in 2:23. True trust involves an entrusting or commitment of oneself to Christ.

I. Antecedents to Belief

"Seeing is believing," we say. However, in John's Gospel seeing may *precede* but not necessarily *produce* believing. It is true that, following the raising of Lazarus, "many of the Jews who . . . had seen what Jesus did, put their faith in him" (Jn. 11:45). However, earlier Jesus said with exasperation, "Unless you people see miraculous signs and wonders . . . you will never believe" (4:48). The author of the gospel apparently both "saw" the Crucifixion (19:35) and "saw and believed" (20:8) the evidence of the empty tomb. To Thomas Jesus uttered the classic: "Because you have seen me, you have believed; blessed are those who have not seen and yet have believed" (20:29).

Seeing is not the only antecedent to belief, but hearing is another. The Samaritans declared, "We have heard for ourselves, and we know . . ." (4:42). Perhaps the hearing aspect is best crystalized in John 5:24—"Whoever hears my word and believes him who sent me . . . has crossed over from death to life."

II. Meaning of Belief

We have already indicated by comparing two forms of the same Greek verb in John 2:23 and 24 that to believe is to commit or entrust oneself. The Amplified Version uses synonyms such as "adhere to, trust in, and rely on." There are other contexts in John where parallel lines shed light on what it means to believe. For instance, John 1:12 has:

> "to all who received him,
>   to those who believed in his name."

Here believing is defined as *receiving*.

Another set of parallel lines are found in John 6:35:

> "He who comes to me will never go hungry"
>   and
> "He who believes in me will never be thirsty."

"Hungry" and "thirsty" stand for spiritual satisfaction. Consequently, to *come to* Christ (as an evangelist might word his invitation in public) is to believe in Christ.

Thirdly, when the Samaritans said, "We have heard . . . and we know that this man really is the Savior of the world" (4:42), are they not really saying, "We have heard . . . and we believe . . ."? Believing seems to involve some *conviction of certainty* about Christ.

III. Witnessing Subjects to Belief

In John's Gospel believing often seems to have both

> SUBJECTS—who "witness" or "testify"
>   and an
> OBJECT—in which belief is placed.

This section will deal with the first—namely, witnesses that bear testimony for bringing people to belief, while the next section will focus upon the object of belief.

John 1:7 indicates that John the Baptist came as a *marturian* to *marturese* (the Greek noun and verb of *martureo*, "to witness").

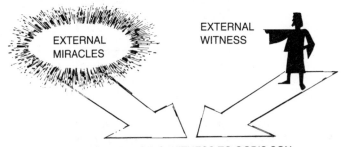

EXTERNAL
MIRACLES

EXTERNAL
WITNESS

BOTH BEARING WITNESS TO GOD'S SON

In Bristol, England, stands the bronze statue of perhaps the greatest Christian hymnwriter of all time—Charles Wesley. Underneath the statue are engraved the words from one of Wesley's hymns—"Oh, let me commend my Savior to you." That is one central commission of a Christian—to commend Christ by way of witness.

What are some means of witnessing that you have found to be winsome and effective?

In John 5 there are five witnesses who (or which) testify to Jesus. They are:

1. Jesus Himself (vs. 31; cf. 8:14);
2. John the Baptist (vss. 32-35);
3. Jesus' works (vs. 36);
4. God the Father (vss. 37, 38; cf. 8:18); and
5. the Scriptures (vss. 39-47).

From elsewhere in John's Gospel we might supplement these with the following witnesses:

6. Jesus' disciples (15:27; 17:20), including the author (19:35; 21:24);
7. other individuals (4:39; 12:17); and
8. the Holy Spirit (15:26).

Thus, all of these become—we might say—the stagehands who stand behind the curtains and shine the floodlight upon the chief character in this divine drama, the Son of God, for He is the:

IV. Worthy Object of Belief

Belief is only as good as the object *of* belief. B. B. Warfield wrote, "It is never on account of its formal nature as a psychic act that faith is conceived in scripture to be saving. . . . It is not, strictly speaking, even faith in Christ that saves, but Christ that saves through faith. The saving power resides exclusively, not in the act of faith or the attitude of faith or the nature of faith, but in the object of faith . . . ."[1]

 Forks and spoons provide no nourishment. Try eating them sometime! However, there is another sense in which forks and spoons do provide nourishment. They are the means, the instruments, by which we take in life-supplying food into our mouths. The vitamins reside completely in the food; nevertheless, an eating utensil conducts the nourishment from the table to the tongue. Food brings life, but a fork brings the food. Faith is the fork necessary for appropriating life, but the saving value of the life resides solely in the food, i.e., in Christ, the Bread of Life.

The centripetal center and magnetic object of a believer's belief is the Faithful One, God's Son. We are to believe "in" Him (Jn. 3:16; 6:35). We are to believe Him (10:38). We are to believe "in his name" (1:12; 2:23; 3:18), His "name" standing for His nature.

In John's Gospel there are embryonic creedal statements. (Creed comes from Latin *credo*, "I believe.") Thus, to believe in Christ is to believe certain things *about* Christ. These appear in John:

1. 4:42—"we . . . believe . . . that this man really is the Savior of the world";
2. 6:69—"we believe . . . that you are the Holy One of God";
3. 9:35—"Do you believe in the Son of Man?";
4. 11:27—"I believe that you are the Christ, the Son of God, who was to come into the world."

Similarly, there are creedlets embedded in I John. For instance,

1. "Jesus is the Christ" (I Jn. 2:22; 5:1);
2. "Jesus is the Son of God" (I Jn. 4:15; 5:5).

Three titles of Jesus are central to John's Gospel. We will study these distinctive titles below.

The Son

"The most conspicuous title of Jesus in the fourth Gospel is neither Son of man nor Son of God but simply the Son, without any modifying phrase."[2] Jesus never used the title "Son of God" for Himself in the first three Gospels. Even the disciples seldom used the title "Son of God" in the Gospels.

 The apostle John in Greek consistently uses "the Son" (*huios*, pronounced *HWEE-ahss*) only for Jesus while reserving the Greek term for "children" (*tekna*) for Christians. This is obscured by the King James Version. For instance, "sons" in John 1:12 should be properly translated "children." This usage is different from Paul, who speaks of believers as both "sons" (Gal. 3:26) and "children."

Leon Morris declared, "Nowhere does He [Jesus] give countenance to the idea that He and others are in the same sense 'sons of God.'[3] This is crystal clear in the personal pronouns of John 20:17, where the risen Lord commands Mary Magdalene: "Go . . . to *my* Father and *your* Father, to *my* God and *your* God."

Jesus' enemies understood by His speaking of God as "my Father" that He was "making himself equal with God" (Jn. 5:18). Furthermore, Jesus never retorted, "Oh, you've misunderstood Me completely; I never intended anyone to think that." No, His acceptance of their accusation meant His acknowledgment of their perception about His claims. It is immediately after John 5:18 that Jesus refers to Himself with the most concentrated clustering of "the Son" references, seven times in John 5:19-23 (and only five more times in the rest of John's Gospel).

Furthermore, "the Son" and "the Father" are obviously correlative ideas. Donald Guthrie asserted, "No other book of the New Testament lays such emphasis on the Fatherhood of God as John's gospel."[4] Guthrie counted 119 usages of "the Father" in John's Gospel. By contrast, "the Father" appears less than 70 times in the Synoptic Gospels. Concerning Jesus' prayer requests in the Upper Room Discourse in John 17:11-25 Guthrie penned: "Nowhere else is the close relationship between Jesus and the Father seen as in these petitions."[5]

? How many items can you list from John 5:19-29 proclaiming what "the Son" or "the Son of God" is able to do? What are they?

The Word

The title "the Word" or "the Word of God" as used for Jesus appears exclusively in John's writings (Jn. 1:1, 14; I Jn. 1:1; Rev. 19:13). Certain thinkers in the ancient world have spoken differently of "the Word." It was used by Greek thinkers like Plato and the Stoics typically to mean *reason* (as in the intelligence that they saw within the universe, or referring to the height of human wisdom).

Philo was a Jew in Alexandria, Egypt who wrote voluminously on the Old Testament. He tried to make the Old Testament compatible with Greek philosophy, so he allegorized much of the Old Testament. He used the title "the Word" over 1300 times. F. F. Bruce wrote, "Philo's *logos* [Greek for "the Word"] is practically identified with the 'intelligible world' conceived in the mind of God as the blueprint for the material world."[6]

In the Old Testament the universe was made "by the word of the Lord" (Ps. 33:6; cp. Gen. 1:3, 6, 9, 14, 20, 24, 26, 29). Furthermore, wisdom is personified in Proverbs 8:12, 22-31 "as the craftsman at his [God's] side" at creation. The personification cannot apply wholesale to Christ, for Wisdom says in Proverbs 8:24—"When there were no oceans, I was given birth."

This is the vat of ideas from which Greek speaking people of that day would have siphoned. Perhaps John 1:18 affords a fragmentary commentary on the meaning of "the Word" by saying concerning the invisible God that the visible Son "has told us all about him" (LB). Jesus is God's interpreter to us who do not speak His language. He has communicated the heart of God to us in a way that no other can. Just as words let us know what another thinks, even so the Word has let us in on God's thinking.

Guido Reni's famous fresco "The Aurora" is painted on the ceiling of the Rospigliosi Palace in Rome. The admirer stands on the floor craning his or her neck to get a look at the breathtaking ceiling painting. However, the palace owner solved the problem of admirers getting stiff necks from the upward gaze. He placed a mirror on the floor in which observers can view the wonders of the painting without looking up.

That is what God the Son does for the invisible God the Father. He has perfectly mirrored for us what God is like.

Ian Macpherson wrote, "Among the thousands thronging Trafalgar Square in London . . . some doubtless look up . . . at the statue of Lord Nelson on top of its colossal column and try to make out what it is really like. In his well-meaning concern to give the famous admiral as exalted a position as possible the sculptor has set him too high to be distinctly discernible from the pavement below. The elevation precludes revelation. At the Ideal Home Exhibition in Olympia in 1948, however, an exact replica in plaster of the figure . . . was placed at eye-level . . . Thus for the first time many had an immediate view of features which before they had only beheld from afar. That is what Jesus did for God."[7]

In John 1:14 we encounter what some have called the most important single verse in the Bible. "The Word became flesh" and (literally) "tabernacled" among us. The great early church leader Augustine said that he could find parallels in pagan philosophers for practically everything in the New Testament except for that saying: "The Word became flesh."

> Veiled in flesh, the Godhead see;
> Hail, the incarnate deity;
> Pleased as man with men to dwell,
> Jesus, our Immanuel."
> —Charles Wesley

In Jesus, deity and humanity are mysteriously conjoined.

 The Incarnation was "that incredible interruption as a blow that broke the very backbone of history."
> —G. K. Chesterton, in James Stewart, *Heralds of God*

His every muscle was a pulley divinely swung, his every nerve divine handwriting, his every bone divine sculpture, his every heartbeat divine pulsation.
> —R. G. Lee, *Beds of Pearls*

Wren expressed himself in granite; Turner expressed himself in oils; Michaelangelo expressed himself in marble; Shakespeare expressed himself in ink; but God selected *flesh* as the ideal vehicle for self-expression. He therefore selected the hallmark of . . . humanity as the supreme vehicle for the revelation of His love.
> —F. W. Boreham, *My Christmas Book*

God

There is no more staggering, awe-inspiring thing one can say about Jesus, the Word, than that He is God. Twice in John's Gospel (three times if one counts the NIV's "God the only Son" in John 1:18) Jesus is directly, unqualifiedly called "God" (Jn. 1:1; 20:28). Christ is "God incarnate," wrote the early Christian church leader Ignatius about A. D. 120. J. E. Davey said, "More explicitly and more emphatically than the other New Testament writers does St. John declare the divinity of Jesus as eternal Son of God and at the same time the distinction between the Son and Father."[8]

John 1:1 provides the building blocks for all Christology:

> In the beginning was the Word,
> and the Word was with God,
> and the Word was God.

In the second clause "the Word" is distinguished from "God," but in the third clause "the Word" is defined as "God." How can these things be? I, a human, cannot be "with" someone and also *be* that someone. Mel Blanc, the great voice actor, is Bugs Bunny, is Porky Pig, is Daffy Duck, is Yosemite Sam, is Jack Benny's Maxwell, etc. But even this example of multiple personality does not afford us an accurate illustration with which to operate.

In three consecutive clauses of John 1:1 we have the amazing truths that:

1. the Son is *coeternal* with the Father (understanding clause one to mean that in the beginning the Word already and always was);
2. the Son is *coexistent* with the Father; and
3. the Son is *coequal* with the Father.

Tony Campolo stated in an interview, "Any person who denies the deity of Christ is not simply denying an interpretation of Scripture, he is denying the exact words of Scripture."[9]

In some important early Greek manuscripts of John 1:18 Jesus is called "*monogenes*" *(mah-know-geh-NACE)* God. The KJV's "only begotten" is inadequate to render this Greek word properly. To illustrate, in Hebrews 11:17 Isaac is spoken of as Abraham's "only son." Now, Bible students know that Isaac was *not* Abraham's only physical son. However, of Abraham's offspring Isaac was unique; he was in a class by himself. Those notions capture what is intended by the Greek word *monogenes* when it is applied to Jesus. Jesus is one of a kind, not to be classified with others. He is in a category all His own. He is the unique un-Xeroxable One! Even among the members of the Trinity, only the Son possesses a glorified body. He is the stallion who bursts all ropes and defies all corrals. Jesus is a species unto Himself. He is "God the One and Only" (Jn. 1:18) who explains and interprets "the only true God" (Jn. 17:3).

At this point a review of this chapter will help us get our bearings. We learn our 3 R's from John:

1. an external REVELATION (or "miraculous sign") is extended for
2. an internal RESPONSE (namely, that we "believe" on the Son of God) for
3. an eternal RESULT (specifically, "eternal life").

ETERNAL RESULT

One of the most important words in John's Gospel (other than names of deity) is the word "Life." The word occurs 36 times in the gospel (more than a quarter of all the New Testament references to life), compared to, say, Romans, with 14 times. John 3:15 is the first mention in this gospel of eternal life. The adjective "eternal" is found 17 times in John's Gospel. Thus, John's Gospel is preeminently the gospel of eternal life.

Matthew, Mark, and Luke speak more about the "kingdom of God," whereas, John's Gospel focuses upon eternal life. However, these are neither opposed nor mutually exclusive ideas. "Eternal life" may sometimes be considered equivalent to the idea of the Kingdom of God. This equivalency may be seen by substituting the phrase "eternal life" for "the kingdom of God" in Jesus' declarations to Nicodemus in John 3:3 and 5. It may also be seen by comparing the use of the two phrases in Matthew 19:16, 17, 29 with 19:23, 24. Both these expressions occur in the context of the disciples' question: "Who then can *be saved?*" (Mt. 19:25). To be "saved" is "to get eternal life" and "to enter the kingdom of God."

Eternal life is not merely present existence stretched like taffy to infinite length. More important than quantity is *quality.* Eternal life resides in having a relationship with God through Christ. This is demonstrated by what may be the closest thing to a New Testament definition of eternal life—John 17:3 ("Now this is eternal life: that they may know you, the only true God, and Jesus Christ, whom you have sent"). This relationship (a fourth "R") comes as we have

the eternal **R**esult ("eternal life") by making
the internal **R**esponse ("believing") as a result of
the external **R**evelations ("Miraculous signs" in John's Gospel).

Eternal life is not restricted to the far-off future. It can be entered now! John 5:24 indicates, "Whoever . . . believes him [God] who sent me [Jesus] has [right now] eternal life and will not [in the future] be condemned; he has crossed over [already in the past] from death to life." The Greek present tense for "has" makes it apparent that the portals of eternal life are entered here and now in the present.

Albert Einstein once commented that we live in an age of perfect means and confused goals. Not so for the knowledgeable Christian!

10

CHRISTIAN HALLMARKS

More Themes in John

One group in the United States calls itself "Christian," but offers literature glorifying Adolf Hitler. Nothing could be sadder than people spewing out hate in the name of Christ. On the other hand, some in modern Christendom seem to feel, "Oh, you worship Baal; how nice!" Teetering on the balance between love and truth can be a precarious perch. Yet the Bible speaks of "truth in love" (Eph. 4:15), as if these need not be mutually exclusive categories. Both of these—truth and love—are leading themes in John's writings.

TRUTH

The word "truth" (and its kinfolk like "true," etc.) is found 59 times in John's Gospel, as compared with a total of 18 times in the preceding three Gospels. The word "truth" is said to have originally conveyed the notion of "without a veil." Thus, truth involves unveiled reality.

Jesus asserted, "I am the way and the truth and the life. No one comes to the Father except through me" (Jn. 14:6). Certain philosophers throughout the centuries have detested Christianity's claim to exclusive truth. Of course, Christianity does not claim that it cannot learn anything from anyone else (see Lk. 16:8, 9; I Thess. 5:21). Nor does it assert that trigonometry must be learned from Scripture. However, it has the responsibility of bringing people to grapple with Jesus' truth claims. Can He forgive sins (in a way others can't) or not? Is He the unique way to God or not?

Some will say that makes Christianity intolerant. Yet in a sense truth is intolerant. The parents of an unattended baby who falls into the swimming pool find—sadly—that the universe does not bend its laws for the baby. The parachutist who bails out of the plane but doesn't pull the rip cord can expect intolerance from the law of gravity. This is no excuse for rigid, uptight, uncaring people who will not listen courteously to the views of others. However, the person who accuses the Christian of intolerance must answer another question: Was Jesus (who claimed John 14:6) a liar? That is the only other logical alternative—unless the Biblical author is the one who has falsely misrepresented what Jesus said.

> Eternal light! Eternal light!
>> How pure the soul must be,
> When, placed within Thy searching sight,
>> It shrinks not, but with calm delight
> Can live and look on Thee.
>> —Thomas Binney

"God is light" (I Jn. 1:5). But what does that pictorial word mean? Turner and Mantey hold: "Physical light connotes 'splendor' or 'glory'; intellectually it connotes 'truth'; morally it connotes 'holiness.' "[1] Therefore, light is a sub-category of, or metaphor for, truth.

The noun "light" is found 23 times in John's Gospel (see 1:7-9; 3:19-21; 5:35; 8:12; 13:30). John tends to be an "either/or" writer.

EITHER	OR
Love	Hate
Light	Darkness
Truth	Lie
Life	Death

 When the famed Dead Sea Scrolls were discovered in the caves at Qumran on the Dead Sea in 1947, they were believed to have been the documents copied by a withdrawn colony of Jewish "monks." Many of those copied scrolls were Old Testament books. However, one non-Biblical scroll was issued under the title of "The War of the Sons of Light with the Sons of Darkness." All of Israel's arch-enemies (e.g., Philistines, Edomites) fall under the umbrella of "Sons of Darkness." This set of polarities are the same as those in John's Gospel.

However, Jesus' attitude was very different from those segregationists at Qumran. Jesus loved Gentiles, Samaritans (racial mongrels), the "riffraff," prostitutes, etc. And Jesus loves Russians, pimps, etc. "Jesus loves the little children—all the children of the world." By contrast, the Qumran colony would have loved to exterminate their enemies. Therefore, "light" and "darkness" in John are not the same as they were for the Dead Sea community.

THE SPIRIT

The words of Jesus make up nearly half of John's Gospel. One such section—almost entirely found only in John's Gospel—is John 13—17 (the so-called Upper Room Discourse). Two phrases capsule the essence of John 1—17. They are:

(1) "He came to that which was *his own*," including the Jewish people (Jn. 1:11). John 1—12 covers Christ's public ministry to His own people.

(2) "Having loved *his own* . . . in the world," including His twelve disciples (Jn. 13:1). John 13-17 covers Christ's private ministry to His disciples.[2]

John 13—17 is the great repository in the Gospels for teaching about the Spirit, who (in light of the theme we've just considered) is called "the Spirit of truth" (Jn. 15:26). The principal Upper Room passages on the subject of the Spirit are John 14:16-18, 26; 15:26; and 16:7-15. Six of the Spirit's roles are treated below.

The Tenant Within

Jesus said in John 7:38, 39—"Whoever believes in me . . . streams of living water will flow from *within* him. By this [pictorial comparison] he meant the Spirit . . . ." Of the Spirit Jesus said in John 14:17—"he lives with you and will be in you." Thus, the Spirit is spoken of as both *with* and *within* a believer. Like a fort attacked from without, Christians have a spring arising from within.

The Personal Tutor

"The Counselor, the Holy Spirit . . . will teach you all things" (Jn. 14:26).

"Outside the [schoolroom] window the bees are droning past, the butterflies flit from flower to flower, and nature seems to cry . . . 'Come play with me.' 'What are you learning, little one?' I say. 'Botany,' is the sad answer. 'We've got to copy these diagrams,' I say . . . 'Come with me.' And presently I teach them more botany by contact with the flowers themselves, than they would have learned by hours of pouring over lesson books."[3]

In the person of the Holy Spirit, a Christian has an actual tenant living within and an animated tutor yearning to teach us the Spirit-inspired Scriptures.

The Defense Lawyer

The word translated "Comforter" in the King James Version or

"Counsellor" in the New International Version (Jn. 14:16, 26; 15:26; and 16:7) is the Greek word *Parakletos (pah-RAH-clay-tahs)*. It is also the same as the "advocate" or "one who speaks . . . in our defense" (I Jn. 2:1). The Greek preposition *para (pah-RAH)* carries the notion of "alongside, beside" as in *paramedic*, i.e., one who comes alongside with medical attention. A *parasite* comes within to weaken the strongest, but the *Paraclete*, the Holy Spirit, comes alongside (and within) to strengthen the weakest person.

> When you're down and out,
>   When you're on the street,
> When evening falls so hard,
>   I will comfort you.
> I'll take your part.
> —Simon and Garfunkel, "Bridge Over Troubled Waters"

The Berkeley Version renders I John 2:1—"We have a Counsel for our defense in the Father's presence." This Defense Attorney is the Son of God, championing our cause. "Nowhere in the pages of history can one find a greater champion of justice," rang out the evangelistic-sounding radio announcer on the old Lone Ranger series. Sorry, Lone Ranger, but this one's got you beat. The Christian's Champion and Defense Lawyer is the Just One, God's Son.

However, the same Greek term is used of God's Spirit. Hence, the Christian has two lawyers—(1) the lawyer within us (the Spirit of God, and (2) the lawyer above us (the Son of God). One lawyer is in our hearts, while the other is also in Heaven.

The Prosecuting Attorney

The Spirit has a dual role. The Spirit is a defense lawyer for the believer, but a prosecuting attorney toward the unbeliever. The verb "convict" in John 16:8 is used outside the Bible in legal contexts for cross-examining. In this sense, the Spirit is a discomforter as well as a comforter. The Spirit's target audience is the world at large. Thus, the heavenly Perry Mason turns His talents toward the guilty:

1. "in regard to sin" (Jn. 16:9) because the chief cause of condemnation is the rejection of Christ;
2. "in regard to righteousness" (Jn. 16:10) because the walking embodiment of righteousness (God's Son) is no longer down here, so the Spirit assumes this role;
3. "in regard to judgment" (Jn. 16:11) because if the leader is already sentenced, what will be the fate of the followers?

The Tour Guide

The Spirit, Jesus promised, "will guide you into all truth" (Jn. 16:13).

 What regions on the map of truth might you want the Tour Guide's guidance for?

The Backstage Hand

Jesus testifies of the Father and the Spirit testifies of Jesus. Just as a backstage hand stands in the shadows and throws the floodlight on the actor on center stage, the Spirit (Jesus said) "will not speak on his own" (Jn. 16:13) but "will bring glory to me" (Jn. 16:14). The Holy Spirit, someone has suggested, is the shy member of the Trinity. The Spirit of God shines the spotlight on the Son of God.

LOVE

In the New Testament there are four Greek words for love. They are:
  (1) *eros (AIR-ahss)*;
  (2) *storge (stohr-GAY)*;
  (3) *philia (fih-LEE-uh)*;
  (4) *agape (uh-GAH-pay)*.

It is from the Greek word *eros* that we derive "erotic" in English. Thus, *eros* love frequently has sexual overtones.

The second word is only found once as a compounded adjective (*philostorgos*) in the New Testament, at Romans 12:10. It has to do with family affection.

Philia (or the verb *phileo*) is used of emotional love, affection, friendship, etc. Its root is seen in the name Philadelphia (brotherly love). We must not undervalue this Greek term, for it is used for (1) Jesus' love for Lazarus (Jn. 11:3), (2) Jesus' love for the beloved disciple, presumably John the apostle (Jn. 20:2), and (3) *even* of the Father's love for the Son (Jn. 5:20). Thus, *philia* and its verbal cohorts are used of deep, warm relationships.

It may even be that the verbs *agapao (ah-gah-PAH-oh)* and *phileo (fil-LEH-oh)* are used interchangeably in John 21:15-17. In Jesus' first two questions to Peter, Jesus used *agapao* in asking Peter if he loved Him. In the third question the text uses *phileo*. Many scholars feel that no special difference is intended by the various use of these two Greek words in this context. On the other hand, Peter consistently uses *phileo* in answering Jesus, and Jesus asks with *phileo* the third time. If a difference in nuance in the two Greek words is intended, it may be that Peter is indicating that he has learned his lesson. Rather than using the full-orbed *agapao*, Peter's has dropped his (typically braggadocious) claim in order simply to stand by his strong affection for Jesus. In that case, Jesus' third question is penetrating, dropping down to Peter's own term: "Peter, do you actually have that strong affection for Me you are claiming?" In other words, Peter isn't willing to claim more than he feels.

Agape is one of the great New Testament words. "Christian love," said William Barclay, "is unconquerable benevolence, invincible good will. It is in fact the power to love the unlovable."[4] In other words, it is not equivalent to the mush, slush, and gush love of pop music drivel. *Agape* love seeks the highest good, or God's best, in the object loved.

Arthur Forte was an old, embittered, unkempt, housebound—virtually chairbound—man. Since he was practically chairbound in one room—and refused to leave the house or go to a hospital—the room smelled badly. Nevertheless, Walter Wangerin visited Arthur regularly. Arthur's helplessness increased until eventually Walter had to dress him. By doing this, Walter confessed that it was here he learned what it meant to be a Christian servant.[5]

THE GREATEST VERSE IN THE BIBLE

It seems fitting to conclude this chapter on the distinctive features of John's Gospel with a study of what is undoubtedly the best known verse by the greatest number of people—John 3:16. Martin Luther called it the "Bible in miniature."

Before turning to the leaves on the John 3:16 tree, so to speak, consider Alexander Maclaren's provocative outline of this famous verse.[6]

I. *The lake: God so loved the world*

II. *The river: He gave His only Son*

III. *The cup: that whoever believes*

IV. *The draught: have everlasting life*

Carnegie Simpson called John 3:16 "the superb commonplace of Christianity." Consider the passion, provision, and purpose of God brought out in this great verse.

I. **The Passion of God Is Shown by the Fact of His Love.**

    A. The Source of Love. "God is love" (I Jn. 4:8, 16). Thus, the whole pyramid of truth about God could properly be turned upside down and funneled into this text. After D. L. Moody heard Harry Morehouse preach again and again on John 3:16, he wrote: "I never knew up to that time that God loved us so much. This heart of mine began to thaw out; I could not keep back the tears. It was like news from a far country: I just drank it in. So did the crowded congregation. I tell you there is one thing that draws above everything else in this world, and that is love."[7] God loves you because that is precisely the kind of God He is.

B. The Stretchingness of Love. "God *so* loved the world." The simple "so" may mark either the manner or the measure of God's love. William Hendriksen paraphrased the manner of God's love as "in such an infinite degree and in such a transcendently glorious manner."[8] In other words, the "so" may answer the question: "how?" Here's how: God *so* loved that He gave.

On the other hand, "so" may carry overtones of "so-o-o-o much" (as a small child might say while stretching her hands in both directions). This is God's eternal yardstick.

> Could we with ink the ocean fill,
>> And were the skies of parchment made.
> Were every stall on earth a quill,
>> And every man a scribe by trade,
> To write the love of God above
>> Would drain the ocean dry,
> Nor could the scroll contain the whole
>> Though stretched from sky to sky."
>> —F. M. Lehman

C. The Significance of Love. Charles Kraft defined love's meaning: "Love is that quality that seeks the best for the recipient at whatever expense to the source."[9] Interestingly, this is the first use of the verb "love" in John's Gospel. Leon Morris noted, "No passage appears to be cited in which any Jewish writer mentions that God loved the world."[10]

D. The Scope of God's Love. God loves *the world*! B. B. Warfield, one of America's greatest theologians, put his finger on the riddle:

> "Do not love the world" (I Jn. 2:15)
> versus
> "God . . . loved the world" (Jn. 3:16).

There is mystery and marvel and miracle in this—that God loves what He tells us not to love!

Of course, we must hasten to point out that the term "world" is used in more than one way in (Scripture and in) John's Gospel. It is used of

1. our physical planet—"He was in the world," i.e., on planet earth; Jn. 1:10a;
2. the people on our planet—"the world did not recognize him" (Jn. 1:10; 3:16);
3. an exaggeration for a majority of the people, as when the Pharisees exclaim, "Look how the whole world has gone after him!" (Jn. 12:19);
4. the whole network of ideas that omits and opposes God and His ways (as in I Jn. 2:15).

E. The Sacrifice of Love. God "gave his . . . Son." Or to elaborate upon this love manifesto as a separate point:

II. The Provision of God to Atone Lies in the Act of His Love.

> The supreme happiness of life is the conviction that we are loved.
> —Victor Hugo

When you care enough to send the very best.
—Hallmark Cards slogan

In Homer's *Iliad* (xxi. 379, 380) the queen of the gods, Juno, says to her offspring, Vulcan: "Dear son, refrain; it is not well that thus a god should suffer for the sake of humans."[11] In this quotation it is as if Juno is checking chapter and verse of her copy of The Greek Deities' Etiquette Manual. In effect, she says: "Wait. Don't do that. Greek gods just don't do that sort of thing. It's not protocol!" By contrast, to be a Suffering Deity (Acts 20:28) *is* protocol, is good etiquette for the true and living God.

"God so loved . . . that he gave . . . ."

In Scripture there is virtually a locked-arms connection between *loving* and *giving*. To love is to give. For example,

"The Son of God . . . loved me and gave himself for me" (Gal. 2:20).
or
"Christ loved us and gave himself up for us" (Eph. 5:2).

Proclaim to every people, tongue, and nation
    That God in whom they live and move is love:
Tell how He stooped to save His lost creation,
    And died on earth that man might live above."
—Mary A. Thompson

Sir Harry Lauder had just lost his son in the great war. In American cities it was customary then for families who had given a son in the war to place a star on the window pane.

A gentleman was walking with his small son down a New York avenue. The boy, who could not have grasped the adult impact of death, was fascinated with counting the stars in the windows. "Oh, look, Daddy," he'd say, "there's another house that has given a son to the war!" "And there's another. Then there's a house with no star at all!"

At last the father and child came to a break between the houses. Through the gap between the roofs could be seen the evening star. In a breathtaking moment of awe the little boy announced, "Oh, look, Daddy, God must have given His Son, because He has a star in His window too."

—F. W. Boreham, A *Handful of Stars*

III. The Purpose of God Is Made Known in the Pact of His Love

"That whoever believes in him shall not perish but have eternal life." God's intention is inclusive and individualized; it's for you!

The universal includes the unit.

—Ian Macpherson, *The Burden of the Lord*

When you hear your own name read out in a will, you prick up your ears. What if there should be something in the testament of our Lord Jesus for you? When I found my own name there, I danced for joy.

—C. H. Spurgeon

> For the love of God is broader
> than the measures of man's mind,
> And the heart of the eternal
> is most wonderfully kind.
> But we make His love too narrow
> by false limits of our own,
> And we magnify its strictness
> with a zeal [God] would not own"
> —Frederick Faber

> "God so loved the world," not just the few,
> The wise, the great, the noble and the true,
> Or those of favored class, or race, or hue;
> "God so loved the world"—do you?
> —Anonymous

11

SYMPHONY OR CACOPHANY?

Relationships Among the Four Gospels

Why are the genealogies in Matthew and Luke so full of completely different names? Why (in the story of the healing of the centurion's servant at Capernaum) does Matthew 8:5-13 present the centurion coming personally to Jesus, while Luke 7:1-10 has the Jewish elders approaching Jesus for the centurion? Isn't this a disagreement in the accounts? Why in the parallel gospel accounts does Matthew (20:29-34) tell of two blind men meeting Jesus' group as they "were *leaving* Jericho" (20:29), while Luke (18:35-43) simply (along with Mark 10:46-52) mentions one blind man, saying it happened "as Jesus *approached* Jericho" (Lk. 18:35)? Surely one must be in error. Can the two possibly be harmonized?

? How would you answer an unbeliever who threw either of the last two Biblical problems at you?

In case you're not sufficiently stumped, what do you do with Matthew 27:9, 10—that quotes Jeremiah as saying they paid 30 pieces of silver for the potter's field? Actually, there is no mention of the price in Jeremiah!

There are two extremes in approaching problems like those specified above. One is to say: "The gospel writers blew it. That's an error." The other extreme is the ostrich head-in-the-sand approach. This approach says, "God inspired it, so let's not tamper with His truth." Or the latter may offer a harmonistic gloss-over that convinces nobody but people who refuse to acknowledge any problems there anyway.

What do we have in the four Gospels—symphony or cacophany? This chapter deals with the thought-provoking question of the interrelationship of the four Gospels. The interrelationships found in the first three Gospels are commonly called the Synoptic Problem. We will handle these difficulties in the four Gospels under three headings: (1) their development, (2) their differences, and (3) their discrepancies.

THEIR DEVELOPMENT

Of Mark's 661 verses only 31 do not appear somewhere in Matthew or Luke.[1] If there is that much overlap, doesn't that make Mark almost optional? For many scholars, the answer to this question lies in the generally accepted order of development of the four Gospels.

? There is obviously a lot of overlap between the Synoptic Gospels. Why do you think God gave us that much repeated material?

If we want *the Gospel* (message) before *the* (written) *Gospels*, chronologically speaking, we turn to other New Testament items that were written before the Gospels were. (Even though the Gospels' material happened first, it is generally agreed that the four Gospels were among the last of the New Testament writings to be recorded.)

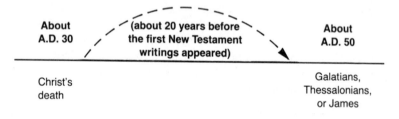

About A.D. 30	(about 20 years before the first New Testament writings appeared)	About A.D. 50
Christ's death		Galatians, Thessalonians, or James

In those 20 years between the Crucifixion and the first written books of our New Testament, we do have a transcription of some of the material that would eventually be included in the Gospels, principally in the preaching of Peter and Paul (in Acts).

PREACHING

Peter (Acts)	Paul (Acts)
chs. 2; 3; 4; 5; 10:34-43	13; 14; 17; 22

 Scholars have studied the sermons of Peter and Paul in order to filter out the common denominator of early Christian preaching. They commonly call this common oral deposit by the Greek word *kerygma* (today usually pronounced *KEH*-rig-muh).

Look up I Thessalonians 1:9, 10. What strands of truth were part of this summation of Paul's early preaching at Thessalonica?

As time passed and the Good News circulated, it took on a "form of teaching" (Rom. 6:17) or "pattern of teaching" (NEB). It is as if the Good News about Jesus began to assume a congealed form or packaging, so as to prevent leakage of any essential ingredients. Paul could urge, "What you heard from me, keep as the pattern of sound teaching" (II Tim. 1:13). Thus, as if he were speaking of a pre-packaged form, Jude (vs. 3) could speak of "the faith [meaning, the basic body of bedrock beliefs that God has] once for all entrusted to the saints."

In several New Testament passages we can detect a movement from the *oral* to the *written* stages of the Christian message.

I JOHN 2:21, 24

1 "the beginning" (when Jesus was here)	2 "what you have heard from the beginning"	3 "I write to you" (2:21)
HISTORICAL HAPPENING	ORAL STAGE	WRITTEN STAGE

HEBREWS 2:3, 4

1 "those [apostles] who heard him" (i.e., Jesus)	2 "confirmed to *us*" [writer and readers] by apostles	3 time of writing of Hebrews

Both authors speak of: (1) the historical happenings (around A.D. 27-30) of Jesus and His disciples; (2) an oral preaching and passage of time (about A.D. 30-50); (3) the written New Testament (about A.D. 50-100). Thus, the "gospel [which] I [Paul] preached" (I Cor. 15:1) involved (I Cor. 15:3, 4):

> Event A ("Christ died")
> Explanation ("for our sins")
> Evidence A ("he was buried," insuring death),
>
> Event B ("he was raised")
> Explanation ("for our justification," Rom. 4:25)
> Evidence B ("he appeared" [vss. 5-8]).

105

This irreducible minimum, these core truths, Paul "passed on" (a technical term for *tradition* in Greek, I Cor. 15:3). Truth packaged as traditional teachings (II Thess. 2:15; 3:6) must be passed on accurately because of the rise of counterfeit or spurious traditions (Col. 2:8; II Thess. 2:2, 3).

In connection with Jesus, His story circulated orally (Acts 1:22; 13:24-39) before being written down. And these sayings of His were passed on, even outside of the written Gospels (Acts 20:35 is an example of one saying of Jesus never found in the four written Gospels). Luke (1:1) even indicates that there were written gospel accounts prior to his written gospel.

By comparing the form of our Gospels, many Bible scholars have concluded that prior to the Gospels being written down, some of the stories about Jesus circulated together orally almost in a congealed, packaged form. This is probably one reason we find a series of stories (like the ones charted below) grouped together around a single theme in more than one gospel.

CONFLICT STORIES

Story	Matthew	Mark
By whose authority?	21:23-27	11:27-33
Parable of vineyard	21:33-46	12:1-12
To give to Caesar or not?	22:15-22	12:13-17
Whose wife (of the seven)?	22:23-33	12:18-27
What's the greatest command?	22:34-40	12:28-34
Who is Messiah?	22:41-46	12:35-37

Above are six conflict-riddled stories (with a question for each) that are arranged in exactly the same order (except Mark has no parallel to Matthew 22:1-4) in two gospels. Does it not stand to reason that early Christian preachers and teachers recited them in just that order before Mark wrote them down that way?

Which of the gospels was published first? The average Christian might assume that Matthew was. However most orthodox scholars tend to believe Mark was launched prior to Matthew. The reasoning for this view is mapped out below.

"If the material in all three gospels is put together, it can be divided into 172 sections. Of these [172] sections Luke contains 127; Matthew 114; Mark 84. Of these sections 48 are peculiar to Luke; 22 to Matthew; 5 to Mark."[2]

Matthew has 1068 verses.

Mark has 661 verses.

Luke has 1149 verses.

Obviously Mark's Gospel is shortest. William Hendriksen has supplied us with the working facts upon which scholars base their theory:

> "Matthew's Gospel contains in substance, almost all of the Gospel according to Mark; in fact, of Mark's 661 verses as many as 606 (about eleven-twelfths) are paralleled in Matthew. Also, slightly more than half of Mark (350 verses—about 53%) is reproduced in Luke.
>
> Stating it differently, the Marcan material . . . in Matthew is compressed into about 500 of the latter's 1,068 verses; hence, amounts to a little less than one-half of that Gospel. Luke's 1, 149 verses have ample room for Mark's 350 verses; in fact, fully two-thirds of Luke's Gospel contains no Marcan material.
>
> ". . . Of Mark's 661 verses only 55 are without parallel in Matthew. However, of these 55 not less than 24 are represented in Luke's Gospel." Therefore, "Mark has only 31 verses which it can strictly call its own."[3]

First of all, it stands to great reason that Mark would have written first rather than have basically recopied Matthew, eliminating a lot and only supplying a grand total of 31 verses uniquely his own. Those who work in office situations know the tendency of memos to get longer rather than shorter, as a rule. Hence, it is easier to believe that Matthew expanded the highly similar Mark rather than that Mark chopped down Matthew and added so little material of his own.

Another factor that argues for believing that Mark is the core document used by Matthew and Luke (rather than vice versa) is presented by Clark Pinnock: "It is a striking fact, that whereas the order of Mark and Matthew may agree against Luke['s order], and the order of Mark and Luke may agree against Matthew['s order], the order of Matthew and Luke never agrees against Mark. In other words, Mark is the stable factor."[4] Therefore, for the reasons traced above, the majority of orthodox Bible scholars hold that the order of writing for the Synoptic Gospels is:

(1) Mark;

(2) Matthew;

(3) Luke.

Someone will undoubtedly at this point raise the question: Why is Matthew first in the order of our Bibles if Mark was actually written first? Probably the main answer here lies in the Book of Matthew's transparent buttonhooking sort of relationship to the Old Testament. One of Matthew's most obvious features is its refrain, "so was fulfilled what the Lord had said through . . ." Consequently, *logically* Matthew . . . comes closest to the Old Testament even if not *chronologically.*

There is a general consensus that the shortest Gospel (Mark) is also the earliest. By comparing almost any of Mark and Matthew's parallel paragraphs, many have come to the conclusion that Matthew must have had Mark's Gospel in front of him as he wrote.

? To look at a similar issue, read and compare Isaiah 2:1-5 and Micah 4:1-5. When we think about how these two passages came to be, what are some possibilities?

As serious Bible students have discussed the relationship existing among the first three Gospels, many have concluded that both Matthew and Luke used Mark's Gospel as one source. Also, many have come to a consensus about a second possibility. Not only are there a bundle of verses in common to Matthew and Mark, but (after subtracting that strand of verses) there is also a group of approximately 250 verses in common between Matthew and Luke that have no parallel in Mark. Naturally, therefore, the question arises: did Matthew and Luke have a second written source for their material in common besides the Gospel of Mark?

As scholars examined the set of 250 verses in common between Matthew and Luke, many of these seemed to fall into the category of *sayings* and sermons of Jesus. (We saw earlier that there were sayings of Jesus circulating outside of our four Gospels proper, namely, Acts 20:35.) This finding caused scholars to wonder if there were not some written collection of Jesus' sayings then circulating that was used by Matthew and Luke as a second source of their gospels. Since many have assumed that such a source was available to Matthew and Luke scholars will speak of Matthew and Luke as using source "Q" (the German word for source is *Quelle*). Now it must be said that no "Q" document has ever been found. Neither if it were found would the document have the title "Q" or "Quelle." However, this view of a circulating collection of Jesus' sayings and sermons has commended itself to the consensus of most Bible scholars.

Now we are ready to grasp the commonly accepted procedure by which the Synoptic Gospels were composed. First, study the diagram:

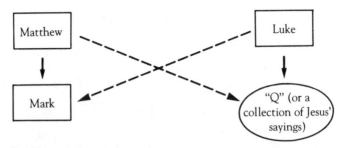

The preceding diagram shows the fairly standard view of how our Synoptic Gospels were composed.

1. Mark was composed first.
2. Matthew used Mark for his basic framework, used "Q," and added his own unique material.
3. Luke used Mark, gathered from "Q," and added his own distinctive material.

FROM THE GOSPEL TO THE GOSPELS

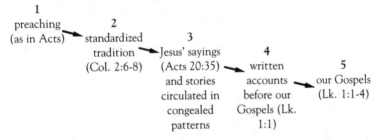

THEIR DIFFERENCES

Now that we have focused on some of the similarities and samenesses in the Gospels and the probable procedure by which they got to be that way, let's focus on some of the differences in the Synoptic Gospels.

Perhaps a good launching pad might be a comparison of the wording on the inscription above Jesus' cross in the four Gospels.

MATTHEW (27:37)	MARK (15:26)	LUKE (23:38)	JOHN (19:19)
"This is Jesus, the King of the Jews"	"The King of the Jews"	"This is the King of the Jews"	"Jesus of Nazareth, the King of the Jews"

? If someone asked you what the inscription above the cross actually said, what would you say? Why do you suppose there are four different wordings?

It becomes perfectly obvious from the preceding wordings of the inscription atop the cross that the Gospel writers are not trying to report verbatim. We might surmise that the fullest reading might have been: "This is Jesus of Nazareth, the King of the Jews." All four include the title "the King of the Jews," which was Pilate's sarcastically slanted indictment.

The majority of Bible scholars hold that Matthew used Mark's Gospel. Yet (assuming this is so) we are intrigued that an apostle and eyewitness of many of the events (Matthew) employed the materials of a nonapostle and noneyewitness (Mark).

? If the last sentence is true, why do you think this would be the case?

One can follow a standard Bible harmony with the Gospel parallels set side by side and observe the alterations Matthew has made on Mark's Gospel. As a tailor of ideas, Matthew clips here, shores Mark up there, adds a patch in another place, inserts a whole layer of cloth in yet another spot. In some places Matthew amplifies considerably (e.g., compare Mark 3:22-30 with Matthew 12:22-32, or Mark 4 with Matthew 13). However, in other places, Matthew abbreviates Mark's account, such as Matthew 8:28-34 in its abbreviation of Mark 5:1-20. Probably in that case it is because Matthew 8 and 9 is a thematic clustering of Jesus' miracles together. Thus, the topic and amount of space would seem to dictate Matthew's tailoring in that case.

We must also keep in mind that a given author's choice for including or excluding some event, saying, or detail may lie in the differing readers' life situations. For instance, earlier we pointed out that only Mark (1:13) includes wild animals in connection with Jesus' temptation. Why? Very possibly because the Roman readership at the very time of Mark's writing (over 20 years after the events happened) was experiencing testing connected with wild animals in the Roman arena. Consequently, Mark's choice of this obscure detail takes on a high degree of relevance if this theory is true.

THEIR DISCREPANCIES

We opened this chapter by raising questions about six discrepancies in the Gospels. In an introductory study such as this one, we cannot grapple with many of the problems raised by comparing the Gospels. However, we can take on a sampling of them so as to be aware of their existence and to suggest avenues that may lead to solutions.

Notice that in the preceding sentence we used the word *may*. There seems to be that mind-set, among some Christians, that we have to have *the* answer to every question. To such people the Bible becomes a kind of vending machine with pop-out answers—if you've just studied hard enough or asked the right Bible teacher. The problem with a lot of these "answers" is that they often don't really answer. Furthermore, the notion of someone being a walking Bible computer full of popout answers is very unappealing to people who know that life is vexed by unanswered and unanswerable questions. *Faith* itself presumes that we have to trust where we do not know complete answers. Only God "knows everything" (I Jn. 3:20).

? Why do you think some Christians feel that they "have to" have an answer for every question?

Read the two quotations by Bible scholars printed below. Many Bible problems are like the relationship between these two quotations.

Charles Pfeiffer[5] said that Babylon was "unquestionably the largest and most magnificent city of the ancient world."

Howard Vos[6] stated that "Babylonia proper was only about the size of New Jersey."

Which writer is wrong? The answer is that neither need be wrong. One statement is about a city's largeness and the other about a territory's smallness. The first quotation is comparing one city to other cities in the ancient world. The second quotation compares an ancient landplot with a modern U.S. state. Both statements can be accurate in light of the frame of reference of each (just as Gal. 6:2 and 5 are compatible).

We must always study the Bible on its own terms, seeking as little as possible to foist our own modern scientific standards upon it. For instance, compare the two synoptic texts below concerning the time of Jesus' transfiguration.

Mark 9:2	Luke 9:28
"after six days"	"about eight days"

In the pre-digital clock world one would see no discrepancy in a set of texts like the two above. Both expressions signify about a week in length. Similarly, this is why on some occasions Jesus' resurrection can be spoken of as taking place "on the third day" (Mt. 20:19; Lk. 18:33) and on other occasions as "after three days" (Mt. 27:63; Mk. 9:31). To modern people the two expressions would signify the third and fourth days respectively. However, ancient peoples would not speak with such

111

modern precision. Therefore, we must understand *them* on *their* terms.

One tool that "solves" many so-called discrepancies is the *representative principle*. This is something inbred into the mentality of the corporate community of Israel. The representative principle is basic to Romans 5:12-21—that the first man was our racial representative in sin. The representative principle is part of the fabric of the mysterious chapter seven of Hebrews—about Melchizedek. The tribe of Levi was represented in their forerunner Abraham, who paid titles to Melchizedek.

When we come to the two Gospel accounts of the centurion's servant (Matthew 8:5-13 and Luke 7:1-10), then, at least one notion of discrepancy disappears. "Did the centurion come himself?" becomes an irrelevant question once we have grasped this Jewish thought form of the *representative principle*. Matthew does not even mention the Jewish elders, but Luke reports that "the centurion . . . sent some elders of the Jews" to Jesus (Lk. 7:3). Thus, the centurion was personally represented in the person of the Jewish elders. Indeed, Luke mentions two sendings by the centurion (7:3, 6). This accords appropriately with the description of a centurion as being one in authority who says to one, "Go," and he goes (Lk. 7:8).

This *representative principle* becomes a mechanism to apply to a number of parallel Gospel accounts where one gospel mentions two figures and another names only one relating in the same story. For example:

Mk. 5:2	Mt. 8:28
one demoniac	two demon-possessed
Mk 10:46 and Lk. 18:35	Mt. 20:30
one blind beggar	two blind men
Mk. 16:5	Mt. 28:5
a young man	one angel

The representative principle assumes that one individual may serve as the representative spokesperson although more than one individual may actually be present. Furthermore, it is frequently Matthew who notes the presence of two individuals whereas the other gospels may only mention one. In his Jewish cast-of-mind Matthew is well aware of the principle enunciated in Deuteronomy 19:15—"A matter must be established by the testimony of two or three witnesses" (cf. Mt. 18:16, 19, 20).

Perspective is another factor that often eases contradictions.

Although not all would buy this solution, some suggest that this is the proper approach with regard to the problem in the two parallel passages cited below.

Matthew 20:29
"As Jesus and his disciples were *leaving* Jericho," they met the blind men.
Luke 18:35
"As Jesus *approached* Jericho, a blind man" was there.

"Can *going* be the same as *coming?*" a critic might ask. No, but putting the two in proper perspective may provide the answer. William Hendriksen commented: "The Roman Jericho of Jesus' day and its present-day ruins lie somewhat to the south of Old Testament or Jewish Jericho. Some have argued . . . that Matthew and Mark are speaking of the Jewish city which Jesus had left, whereas Luke is speaking of the Roman, at which Jesus had not yet arrived." Nevertheless, Hendriksen went on to acknowledge, "we do not now have the solution to the problem."[7] Sometimes it's best to say, "I'm just not sure."

Matthew 27:9, 10 provides a difficulty for modern readers in quoting the betrayal price of Jesus as if it were to be found in Jeremiah. Yet Jeremiah contains no quotation that specific. Probably the best available solution here is that the specific sum is found in Zechariah 11:13, and the Jewish Talmud placed Jeremiah first in the order of the prophetic books. In that case, Zechariah (11:13) would come under the general heading supplied by the lead book in the series, namely, Jeremiah.

This solution, of course, requires us to dismiss our own modern preconceptions about what should be there and attempt to understand the Biblical writings from the mind-set of the people who wrote them. This is a cardinal principle of all Biblical interpretation. We must seek to *expose* what they intended rather than *impose* what we expect.

So pursue this track relentlessly. Happy interpreting!

CHAPTER
12

SAME STORY, DIFFERENT DESIGN
The Gospels Categorized and Compared

From time to time something seemingly brand-new hits the market. It may be a hula hoop, a yo-yo, a Frisbee, a skateboard, an Edsel, or a Cabbage Patch doll. For who-knows-what-reason, these items create a sensation, so that each one is a phenomenon, a thing-unto-itself. Some are so unique (like the Edsel) that they bomb out altogether. Others—like the Cabbage Patch dolls among thousands of other dolls—become top sellers. Each of these created a niche for itself.

Something similar takes place in literature. Literary forms take on a certain distinguishable group of characteristics (just as a Nash Rambler or Cabbage Patch doll has distinguishable characteristics). A short story is distinguishable from an epic poem. Poetry is distinguishable from prose. In literature a distinguishable form with its own set of characteristics is called *genre* [ZSHAN-ruh]. Similarly, in the world of televiewing, a sit-com (situation comedy) is distinguishable from a documentary.

Many longtime Bible students are unaware of it, but the Gospels are a *genre* in themselves. "The Gospel is Christianity's contribution to literary types. It is without doubt the most effective literary form of religious expression that has ever been devised."[1]

Imagine the librarian at the world-famous library of ancient Alexandria being handed a copy of the New Testament Gospels for the first time. Imagine the librarian scratching his head as he pondered his master sheet with (whatever corresponded to) his Dewey decimal system of library classification. On what shelf would he put this new acquisition? Would he put it with Plutarch's *Lives*? No. Would he classify it with Socrates' *Memoirs*? No. There really was no known precise category into which the librarian might slot it. In a way it

114

deserved to be put on a shelf all its own, for it was the sole invention of Christianity. Thus at the time of their origination, the Gospels were a genre unto themselves.[2]

 Why might we hesitate simply to classify the Gospels among the biography section of a library? What makes the Gospels different from most biographies?

In the Introduction we spoke of the gospel writers as four painters, each giving his rendering of the same subject but from a different perspective. Naturally, because of this unique interrelationship, the four Gospels may be compared and contrasted in a multitude of ways. For a starting point the most obvious difference is the marked divergence of the three Synoptic Gospels from the Gospel of John. Some of the variations are charted below.

MATTHEW, MARK, AND LUKE	JOHN
Galilean Gospels	Judean Gospel
Career of the earthly historical Jesus (focuses on the historical, running narrative of Jesus' public ministry)	Concept of the eternal, heavenly Word and Son (focuses on deity)
Structured more around actions	Spotlights seven miraculous signs and long speeches
More obviously concerned with the chronological	More obviously framed around theological
Story starts in Bethlehem (except for Mark)	Gospel launched from eternity

In most cases these differences are purely a matter of emphasis (rather than of elimination). For example, the Gospel of John does not altogether omit chronology (in fact, feast dates are very prominent in John), but we do not get the same down-to-earth feel of calendar routine from John's Gospel that the beginning reader would from the first three.

What might the similarity of the first three Gospels as contrasted with John teach us about the make-up of the Christian Church? Name and describe appreciatively one Christian you know who is very un-run-of-the-mill.

115

SOME ONLIES IN JOHN'S GOSPEL

The title "the Word" is used for Jesus *only* in John.

Jesus is explicitly and directly called "God" *only* in John (of the four Gospels—Jn. 1:1; 20:28).

The cleansing of the Temple is placed at the beginning of Jesus' ministry *only* in John (2:13-17).

Nicodemus is found *only* in John's Gospel (3:1-15; 7:50, 51; 19:39).

The Samaritan woman is *only* in John (4:1-42).

The raising of Lazarus (ch. 11) is *only* in John's Gospel.

The full-orbed, first Resurrection appearance to Mary Magdalene is found *only* in John (20:2-18).

? Why do you think John is so different from the other three Gospels?

Once we have attempted to see how different John's Gospel is from the Synoptic Gospels (and one way to do that is to compare the column on John's Gospel with the others in a standard Harmony of the Gospels), we must move on to discern distinctions in emphases in the three Synoptic Gospels. (For review, what does "Synoptic" mean?) Do you ever mix up Goodyear and Goodrich, Arminians and Armenians? When resemblances are remarkable and when our level of acquaintance with a person or product is low, it's easy to get two items or individuals confused. However, no one working for Goodyear will get their product mixed up with Goodrich—because that person has had ample opportunity to get acquainted with which is which.

How do we determine the distinctives among the first three Gospels? Some ways of determining distinctiveness are:
1. the principle of selectivity. What an author includes or omits may aid us in detecting why he wrote;
2. the principle of recurrence. If certain words or expressions keep cropping up (e.g., "the kingdom of heaven" only in Matthew), we may ask why this is so;
3. the principle of stated purpose. If a writer has clearly written *why* he has written (Lk. 1:1-4; Jn. 20:30, 31), our task is lightened and enlightened.

First, let's compare the way a few scholars have compared the Synoptic Gospels:

> "Matthew is the most theological Gospel,
> . . . Mark is the most chronological, and
> . . . Luke is the most personal."
> —Charles Ryrie[3]

> Matthew's focus: What did Jesus say? (to Jews)
> Mark's focus: What did Jesus do? (for Romans)
> Luke's focus: Where did Jesus come from (for philosophical Greeks)
> —Ralph Earle[4]

> Matthew - the coming of the promised Savior
> Mark - the life of the powerful Savior
> Luke - the grace of the perfect Savior
> John - the possession of the personal Savior
> —Griffith Thomas[5]

SOME "IF"FY ISSUES CHARTED

Gospel	When written	Where written from
Matthew	c. A.D. 55-60	Antioch in Syria?
Mark	early 50's	Rome
Luke	c. A.D. 60-65	Rome (Robert Gundry) Caesarea (Graham Scroggie)

At this point, then, we are ready to recap our findings from the four Gospels. Once more we will summarize the distinctive features of each gospel (in the order of publication that is generally accepted).

MARK

Mark is an action-packed gospel for Roman readers about the serving Son of God, bearing Peter's stamp.

I. Its Action

Mark is a fast-paced, action-packed treatment primarily of the actions of Jesus. "Immediately" is a favorite word (42 times) and the conjunction "and" is used to join sentences and statements around 400 times in Mark. Mark likes using the Greek present tense so as to make the reader feel he or she is watching the action happen.

117

As compared with Matthew, Mark prefers Jesus' works to His words. Mark has no Sermon on the Mount (like Matthew and Luke). Nor does Mark include any birth narratives for Jesus (like Matthew and Luke). To keep up with Mark, get out your jogging shoes.

II. Its Audience

Mark is geared for Roman readers. Therefore, to appeal to his audience, Mark presents the character of Jesus in its full-orbed strength. Christ is the undaunted controversialist in Mark. To some extent Mark tips his hand as to his readership by the amount of Latin loan words that jut out of the path of his gospel—more than in any other book in the New Testament.

So as not to confuse his readers with Roman law, Mark omits the word "law" altogether (as Jews would use it). Also we find included in Mark 15:21 an individual who was evidently well-known to the Roman church (see Rom. 16:13).

III. Its Accent

Mark accentuates Jesus' role as Son of God and Servant. The very first verse of Mark's Gospel announces "the Gospel about Jesus Christ, the Son of God." Mark's Son of God also serves (Mk. 10:45). In the very last verses in the Authorized Version, we see the risen Son who "worked with" His followers as they carry out His commission.

IV. Its Apostolic Overtones

Scholars generally agree that behind Mark stands his spiritual father (I Pet. 5:13), Peter. At least seven of the early church leaders after the apostles link Mark with Peter. Thus, the indelible imprint of the apostle Peter is branded upon Mark's Gospel.

MATTHEW

Matthew is the fullest gospel for Jewish readers with Old Testament flavor and five sections of Jesus' teaching.

I. Its Target

While Luke's Gospel is longest in sheer number of verses, Matthew's Gospel provides a fullness to Jesus' systematic sections of teaching. Apparently using Mark's Gospel for his chronological framework, Matthew inserts five chunks of Jesus' lengthy teaching (with concluding formulas) at various intervals in his gospel.

Matthew's prime target is his own Jewish people. Matthew himself was the walking embodiment of the tension of his world—a Jew taking money from Jews for their non-Jewish conquerors. Therefore, his burden is to show how Jesus is the fulfillment of Old Testament prophecy. This Matthew does by the recurring formula—"this took place to fulfill what the Lord had said through the prophet" (Mt. 1:22; cf. Mt. 2:5, 6; 2:15; 2:17, 18; 2:23; 4:14-16; 8:17; 12:17-21; 13:35; 21:4, 5; 26:31; 26:54; 26:56; and 27:9, 10). Matthew quotes the Old Testament Scriptures over 40 times.

If we only focused on one strand of verses in Matthew (1:21; 10:5, 6; 12:6; 15:24), we might conclude that Matthew had turned Jewish bigot or that Jesus was racist. However, Matthew's Gospel offers within its full-fledged embrace the Good News about Messiah to Gentiles on an equal footing (Mt. 2:1-12; 4:15, 16; 8:10, 11; 12:21; 15:21, 22; 21:43; 24:14; 28:18-20).

No doubt for supersensitive Jewish readers Matthew has frequently resorted to the expression "the kingdom of heaven," found only in his gospel.

Money-conscious Matthew (only in Matthew are the parables of 18:21-35 and 20:1-16 and the money miracle of 17:24-27) had also been race-conscious Levi. He had turned traitor by tax collecting as far as his race was concerned, but he ended up bringing them *gratis* the greatest gift of all—the Messiah for Jews and Gentiles alike.

II. Its Teaching

Into the overall framework of Mark's Gospel Matthew lowered five sections of cargo. That cargo contained over 300 verses located nowhere else. Matthew supplies five sets of systematic teaching of Jesus closing with a formula like "When Jesus had finished saying these things" (7:28). The five blocs of teaching that conclude with that formula are:
1. the Sermon on the Mount (in its classic form in Mt. 5-7; cf. 7:28 for formula);
2. the Disciples' Commission (Mt. 10; cf. 11:1);
3. the Parables of the Kingdom (Mt. 13; cf. 13:53);
4. Instructions to the Church (Mt. 18; cf. 19:1);
5. the Olivet Discourse (Mt. 24, 25; cf. 26:1).

Also, only Matthew gives us Jesus' long tirade against the scribes and Pharisees, in its complete form, in chapter 23 (although that address has no formula ending like the other five).

In Matthew's version of the Sermon on the Mount, Jesus—the new Moses—audaciously announced His authority by declaring six times, "You have heard that it was said . . . but I tell you" (or a similar expression in 5:21, 22; 5:27, 28; 5:31, 32; 5:33, 34; 5:38, 39; and 5:43, 44). Not only is Jesus represented as greater than Moses by Matthew, but Matthew alone (in 12:6) asserts that "one greater than the temple is here." Thus, Matthew is written by an unorthodox Jew to orthodox Jews about an unorthodox Jewish Messiah.

LUKE

Luke is the beautiful literary gospel with unforgettable parables, emphasizing the poor, women, prayer, and the Spirit.

I. His Style

Luke 1:1-4	very Greek
Luke 1:5—2:52	Hebrew cloaked in Greek
Luke 3—24	very Greek

Of the four Gospels, Luke's betrays the most cultivated Greek literary style of writing (except for much of the early material in Luke 1:5—2:52, pulled probably from firsthand interviews in Palestine).

Like the great Greek historians (e.g., Thucydides), Luke began his narrative with a clear-cut statement of purpose. Like a doctor anxious to diagnose accurately, Luke painstakingly researched his source material. Of the four Gospels, Luke is the only one to date his history by the Roman emperors (Lk. 2:1; 3:1).

II. His Storytelling

Some of literature's classic parables are couched in Luke's Gospel. Luke 6:12—8:3 and 9:51—18:13 contains a breakaway section from the other three Gospels. Consequently it is in Luke's midsection (chaps. 10—18) that we find some of the world's greatest parables.

Among Luke's unforgettable parables are:
1. the Good Samaritan (10:25-37);
2. the Rich Fool (12:13-21);
3. the Lost Coin (15:8-10);
4. the Prodigal Son (15:11-32);
5. the Rich Man and Lazarus (16:19-31—is it a parable?);
6. the Tax Collector and the Pharisee (18:9-14).

Furthermore, only Luke preserves for us two parables on persistent praying—the Friend at Midnight (11:5-10) and the Widow and the Unjust Judge (18:1-8).

III. His Social Stress

The Jesus in Luke's Gospel is the great Equalizer. Mary's Magnificat

(Lk. 1:46-55) is a most revolutionary document. Here God is the Leveler who brings down the high and brings up the lowly.

Consequently, Luke's Gospel contains more about the poor than do the other three Gospels. Mary and Joseph fall into the category of the poor—by virtue of the type of sacrifice they offer in the Temple (2:24). Jesus' inaugural sermon announced His "good news to the poor" (4:18). Unlike Matthew in his beatitudes, Luke doesn't spiritualize. Luke simply says, "Blessed are you who are poor" (6:20). In the story of the rich man and Lazarus (16:19-31), the poor man is comforted in the afterlife while the rich one ends in torment. Luke gives us the great reversal.

Women come to the forefront in Luke as they do in no other gospel. At least 13 women are named by Luke that are not found in the other Gospels. Among them are Elizabeth (ch. 1), Anna (ch. 2), and Joanna and Susanna (8:3), who help subsidize Jesus' itinerant ministry. We find Luke making the same emphasis in Acts (see Acts 1:14; 2:17, 18; 9:36-41; 16:14-18; 17:4). If John Robinson could call Luke "Paul's Boswell" (*Redating the New Testament*), then Paul was Luke's Samuel Johnson. And Paul showed this same tendency (Rom. 16:1, 7 ["Junias" may well be a woman apostle]; Gal. 3:28).

Luke's Gospel recognizes those on the fringes of society. Samaritans appear on three occasions (9:51-56; 10:33; 17:16) where they are found in none of the other Gospels. Only Luke includes the touching story of the loving ex-prostitute (7:36-50).

Luke exhibits a fondness for the detested tax collector (15:1, 2), and only Luke provided us with the transformation of Zaccheus, chief tax collector at Jericho (19:1-10). Likewise, Luke alone included in his account the fuller story of the repentant thief on the cross (23:39-43).

However, Jesus cannot be accused of reverse discrimination, for on three occasions in Luke's Gospel He dines with Pharisees (7:36; 11:37; 14:1). Sir Thomas More was called in the famed play "A Man for All Seasons." Jesus is the God-Man for all strata of people in Luke's rendition.

IV. His Spiritual Stress

While conservatives often downplay social needs, liberals often underplay spiritual emphases. By contrast, Luke goes to both ends of the pendulum. Luke's spiritual stress is seen in the distinctive role he gives to the Holy Spirit, prayer, praise, rejoicing, songs, and the Temple.

The Holy Spirit, mentioned 53 times in Luke-Acts, is referred to more often in Luke's Gospel than in either of the first two Evangelists. There are seven such references in the first two chapters alone. Jesus was conceived within Mary's womb by the agency of the Holy Spirit (1:35). Three senior citizens in Luke 1 and 2 speak from the Spirit-as-a-source (1:41, 67; 2:25-27). The Spirit is operative both in Jesus' attesting (3:22) and testing (4:1, 14).

The human counterpart to the unleashed Spirit (see Acts 4:31) may be said to be prayer. Luke's is peculiarly the gospel of prayer. There are seven occasions when Luke alone shows us Jesus in prayer. Only Luke mentions Jesus in prayer at His baptism (3:21) and transfiguration (9:28). Jesus spent all night in prayer prior to choosing the 12 apostles.

Praise and rejoicing leap up like a gurgling brook in Luke's Gospel. The expression "praising God" is contexted in Luke more often than in all the rest of the New Testament writings together. The last two verses of Luke find the disciples returning "with great joy" and "praising God" (24:52, 53).

Five spiritual songs are found only in Luke 1 and 2 among the Gospels. They are:
1. Elizabeth's Benedictus (1:42-45);
2. Mary's Magnificat (1:46-55);
3. Zechariah's Song (1:68-79);
4. the angels' Gloria in Excelsis (2:14); and
5. Simeon's Nunc Dimittis (2:29-32).

No wonder, with all of this spiritual floodtide that the Temple is "the epicenter of Luke's Gospel." Luke launches from the Temple (1:9-11) and lands there again in its closing verses (24:53).

JOHN

In John's Gospel miraculous signs are intended to inspire belief in the Son for eternal life.

I. Seven Signs

John's Gospel is structured around seven miraculous signs of Jesus:
1. water to wine (2:1-11);
2. nobleman's son healed (4:46-54);
3. Bethesda pool healing (5:1-15);
4. feeding of over 5000 (6:1-15)—the one miracle recorded in all four Gospels;
5. walking on water (6:16-21);
6. healing the man born blind (9:1-12);
7. raising Lazarus (11:1-46).

Of course, Jesus' resurrection is an eighth miraculous sign, serving as the crown and capstone to them all.

II. Seven Sayings

Although John's Gospel contains the "I am" title of Jesus numerous times, there are seven times when the "I am" title has a predicate attached to it. These seven are:

1. "I am the bread of life" (6:35);
2. "I am the light of the world" (8:12);
3. "I am the gate [door]" (10:9);
4. "I am the good shepherd" (10:11);
5. "I am the resurrection and the life" (11:25);
6. "I am the way and the truth and the life" (14:6);
7. "I am the vine" (15:5).

III. Seasonal Structure

Of the four Gospels, John's is the most conscious of the Jewish red-letter days. Those mentioned in John are:

1. Jesus' first adult Passover (2:23);
2. "a[n unnamed] feast of the Jews" (5:1);
3. a second "Jewish Passover Feast" (6:4);
4. "the Jewish Feast of Tabernacles" (7:2);
5. "the Feast of Dedication" or Hanukkah (10:22); and
6. Jesus' final Passover (12:1; 13:1).

IV. Spiritual Staples

Two terms that are crucial to John's Gospel are:

"believe"

"eternal life."

John never uses the noun "faith." Instead, John uses his favorite verb "believe" close to 100 times. To believe is to rely upon, trust in, and commit oneself to the Son of God. Another key word (perhaps the most important word in the entire gospel) is "Life." John 3:15 is the first reference to "eternal life" in John.

V. Soaring High

John lifts us into the eternal ether. Immediately we go soaring back, back, back to eternity with one of the most staggering statements:

> In the beginning was the Word,
> and the Word was with God,
> and the Word was God.

John's Gospel launches from the assumption that Jesus "was God" (1:1) and soars to Thomas's climactic confession, "My Lord and my God!" (20:28).

 If Jesus Christ be God, there is no sacrifice too great to make for Him.
—C. T. Studd

NOTES

Chapter 1
[1] Harold St. John, *An Analysis of the Gospel of Mark* (London: Pickering and Inglis Ltd., 1956), p. 18.
[2] Graham Scroggie, *Guide to the Gospels* (London: Pickering and Inglis Ltd., 1948), p. 168.

Chapter 2
[1] in Bruce Shelley, *Church History in Plain Language* (Waco, TX: Word, 1982), p. 329.
[2] George Ladd, *A Theology of the New Testament* (Grand Rapids, MI: Eerdmans, 1974), pp. 161, 162.
[3] Ladd, Ibid., p. 162.
[4] Alfred Edersheim, *The Life and Times of Jesus the Messiah, II* (Grand Rapids, MI: Eerdmans, 1959), 75.
[5] Ladd, *A Theology of the New Testament*, p. 165.
[6] B. B. Warfield, *The Lord of Glory* (Grand Rapids, MI: Zondervan), p. 82.
[7] F. F. Bruce, *The Book of Acts* (Grand Rapids, MI: Eerdmans, 1954), p. 188.

Chapter 3
[1] Scroggie, *A Guide to the Gospels*, p. 247.
[2] Ralph Martin, *New Testament Foundations, I* (Grand Rapids, MI: Eerdmans, 1975), 227.
[3] Scroggie, *A Guide to the Gospels*, p. 267.
[4] E. Schuyler English, *R. G. Lee* (Grand Rapids, MI: Zondervan, 1949), p. 387.
[5] F. W. Boreham, *A Bunch of Everlastings* (Philadelphia: Judson Press, 1952), pp. 130, 131.

Chapter 4
[1] William Barclay, *Introduction to the First Three Gospels* (Philadelphia: Westminster Press, 1966), p. 148.
[2] Lorman Petersen, *The Zondervan Pictorial Encyclopedia of the Bible, IV* (Grand Rapids, MI: Zondervan, 1975), p. 121.

Chapter 5
[1] Edersheim, *Life and Times, I*, p. 582.
[2] Walter R. Bowie, *The Interpreter's Bible, IV* (Nashville, TN: Abingdon, 1952), p. 169.
[3] *Communication-Learning for Churchmen, I* (Nashville, TN: Abingdon, 1968), p. 106.
[4] in John Broadus, *An American Commentary on the New Testament: Matthew* (Valley Forge, PA: American Baptist Pub. Society, 1886), p. 284.
[5] G. Henry Hubbard, *The Teachings of Jesus in Parables* (Boston: Pilgrim Press, 1907), p. xvi.
[6] Donald Grey Barnhouse, *God's Heirs* (Wheaton, IL: VanKampen Press, 1953), p. 112.
[7] William Barclay, *And Jesus Said* (Philadelphia: Westiminster Press, 1970), p. 95.
[8] Merrill Tenney, *The Wycliffe Bible Commentary* (Chicago: Moody, 1962), p. 1054.
[9] *Looking Ahead*, June, 1987.
[10] A. T. Robertson, *Word Pictures in the New Testament, II* (Nashville, TN: Broadman, 1931), p. 209.

Chapter 6
[1] adapted from Earle Ellis, *The Gospel of Luke* (Grand Rapids, MI: Eerdmans, 1966), p. 67.
[2] Scroggie, *A Guide to the Gospels*.

Chapter 7

[1] William Hendriksen, *The Gospel of Luke* (Grand Rapids, MI: Baker, 1978), p. 853.
[2] Alfred Plummer *The International Critical Commentary: St. Luke* (New York: Charles Scribner's Sons, 1896), p. 433.
[3] William Manson, *The Gospel of Luke* (New York: Richard R. Smith, Inc., 1930), p. 209.
[4] Edersheim, *Life and Times, II*, p. 353.

Chapter 8

[1] Steven Barabas, *The Zondervan Pictorial Bible Dictionary* (Grand Rapids, MI: Zondervan, 1963), p. 280.
[2] Ethelbert Stauffer, *Jesus and His Story* (New York: Knopf, 1959), p. 174.
[3] Leon Morris, *The Gospel According to John* (Grand Rapids, MI: Eerdmans, 1971), p. 437.
[4] in William Barclay, *The Letter to the Romans* (Philadelphia: Westminster Press, 1954), p. v.

Chapter 9

[1] B. B. Warfield, *Biblical and Theological Studies* (Philadelphia, Presbyterian and Reformed, 1952), pp. 424, 425.
[2] Barker, Lane, and Michaels, *The New Testament Speaks* (New York: Harper and Row, 1969), pp. 402, 403.
[3] Leon Morris, *The Lord from Heaven* (Grand Rapids, MI: Eerdmans, 1958), p. 34.
[4] Donald Guthrie, *Zondervan Pictorial Encyclopedia, III* (Grand Rapids, MI: Zondervan, 1975), p. 624.
[5] Guthrie, *Ibid.,* p. 625.
[6] F. F. Bruce, *Commentary on the Epistles to the Ephesians and Colossians* (Grand Rapids, MI: Eerdmans, 1957), p. 197.
[7] Ian Macpherson, *Burden of the Lord* (New York: Abingdon Press, 1955), p. 14.
[8] in Ladd, *A Theology of the New Testament*, p. 251.
[9] Tony Campolo, *Christianity Today,* September 20, 1985.

Chapter 10

[1] George Turner and Julius Mantey, *The Gospel of John* (Grand Rapids, MI: Eerdmans, 1964), p. 28.
[2] Adapted from Barker, Lane, and Michaels, *The New Testament Speaks*, p. 404.
[3] F. B. Meyer, *Gospel of John* (London: Marshall, Morgan, and Scott, 1950), p. 288.
[4] William Barclay, *More New Testament Words* (New York: Harper and Brothers, 1958), pp. 15, 16.
[5] *The Observer*, December, 1982.
[6] in Griffith Thomas, *Ministerial Life and Work* (Chicago: Bible Institute Colportage, 1927), p. 155.
[7] William Revell Moody, *The Life of Dwight L. Moody* (New York: Revell, 1900), p. 127.
[8] William Hendriksen, *The Gospel of John, I*, p. 139.
[9] Charles Kraft, *Communication Theory for Christian Witness*, p. 23.
[10] Morris, *The Gospel According to John*, p. 229.
[11] in Turner and Mantey, *The Gospel of John*, p. 97.

Chapter 11

[1] Barclay, *First Three Gospels*, p. 86.
[2] Barclay, Ibid., p. 215.
[3] William Hendriksen, *The Gospel of Matthew* (Grand Rapids, MI: Baker, 1973), p. 6.
[4] Clark Pinnock, *Zondervan Pictorial Encyclopedia, I*, p.788.
[5] Charles Pfeiffer, *Old Testament History* (Grand Rapids, MI: Zondervan, 1973), p. 428.
[6] Howard Vos, *Effective Bible Study* (Grand Rapids, MI: Zondervan, 1956), p. 127.
[7] Hendriksen, *The Gospel of Luke*, p. 842.

Chapter 12

[1] Edgar Goodspeed, *Introduction to the New Testament* (Chicago: University of Chicago Press, 1937), p. 125.

[2] C. F. Evans, *The New Testament Gospels* (London: British Broadcasting Corporation, 1965), pp. 7ff.

[3] Charles Ryrie, *A Biblical Theology of the New Testament* (Chicago: Moody), p. 27.

[4] Ralph Earle, *Zondervan Pictorial Encyclopedia, IV*, p. 80.

[5] Griffith Thomas, *Outline Studies in the Gospel of Matthew* (Grand Rapids, MI: Eerdmans, 1961), p. 14.

DIRECTIONS FOR GROUP LEADERS

The questions and projects below should form the framework of the actual time spent in group discussion. The week before every class the leader ought to assign both the lesson and the Bible passage (found under each chapter title) to be read for the upcoming class so that students will come to class with an informational foundation for the discussion.

Some class members may come without having read the lesson for the week. It would be wise to have a plan for including them in a short review session before jumping into the study proper. Perhaps two or three other class members could give an "overview report" with highlights from the reading. Certain portions of the book could be read aloud. Or, you could set up a short dialogue session between two who have read the lesson content. However you do it, make sure the unprepared members feel every bit as important to the class as the others.

The New International Version, 1984 edition, is the Bible translation quoted throughout the commentary, although the study can be conducted using any helpful translation. Remember to read the directions for each chapter at least a week before class. That way, you will have adequate time to pull together some of the special learning experiences requiring advance preparation.

To encourage group discussion, don't be shy about asking, "Susan, in what ways has this issue been a part of your own life experience?" If someone responds to a question, you can add something like, "How have others of you dealt with this?"

Don't be afraid of respectful disagreement, for we can learn from people who differ from us. Even if you don't agree, you can comment, "I don't think I agree, but it will certainly give us something to think about. How do others of you feel?" The secret of effective group discussion is to keep throwing open-ended questions (*not* questions that can be answered with a mere"yes" or "no") back to members of the group. Be sure to acknowledge people's contributions: "Thanks for sharing that, David. I know it took some courage to bring that up."

Try to include in all your group sessions some of the key ingredients for building group life: a time for sharing, a time for prayer, and perhaps light refreshments around which significant conversation can take place. Bible study groups can be much more than just an intellectual trip. They can become a means of developing strong bonds of Christian fellowship.

Below, three items will be found for each of the 12 class sessions:

A. A Need-hook. Each week this paragraph will provide a discussion item with which to open class. Normally it will try to hook into some felt need humans experience that will in turn tie into a major truth emerging from the Bible passage to be studied. Hence, the leader moves the class from a felt need to the Bible principles.

B. Fun Feature(s). Every week the leader is provided with an activity (to do or discuss) with an element of group action or even humor involved. This group game or project will sensitize the students to an idea or issue from the particular passage being studied.

C. For Group Discussion. While there are usually a number of questions included within the body of the commentary at pertinent points in the flow of the study, seven to ten extra application questions on each given Bible passage are supplied here. The leader should allow plenty of time for students to think about and respond to the questions. If all questions and activities are used, the class time will probably take about an hour (although by selectivity in the use of the questions, the class time could be made shorter).

Happy study and good grouping to you!

CHAPTER 1

A. A Need-hook

Let the class play amateur marketers. Divide the class into small groups. Let each small group take one of the following audiences and tell how they would gear the Gospel toward that audience.

1. yuppies (i.e., young, upwardly mobile, city types)
2. skid-row transients
3. young feminists
4. macho construction workers
5. homosexuals
6. ghetto-trapped youngsters

After each group representative shares how their group decided to zero in on their targeted audience, move to how Mark's Gospel is slanted to Roman readers.

B. Fun Features

1. Bring in an old homemade movie. After showing a part of it, make the comparison of Charlie Chaplin movies with Mark's fast-moving pace in his gospel.

2. Let class members talk about their own homemade movies (or their friends') prior to turning to Mark's rapid-moving, movielike quality.

3. Let small groups race each other to see how many foreign words they can come up with that have been taken over directly into English (e.g., tortilla and other food words). Then shift to how Mark has numerous Latinisms and Aramaisms.

C. For Group Discussion

1. Can you recall some time when you (like Mark) felt particularly excited about the Christian Gospel? What person epitomizes that sense of excitement for you?

2. In what ways does one's excitement for something—or one's priorities—have upon mannerisms, body language, conversation, etc? (From there move to how Mark's excitedness comes out in conjunctions, verb tenses, etc.)

3. On an index card write down: What are the essentials of the Christian message? Discuss what the class as a whole has written? What did they have in common? What was left out? What *should be* left out? Or added? Back up your answers with Biblical support.

4. Do you tend to run from controversy? Give an example of when you faced controversy head on. What happened? Do you think church people tend to repress discussing problems under the guise of unity? What can be done?

5. How do you think Dale Carnegie (*How to Win Friends and Influence People*) might rate Jesus?

6. In what ways do you think Jesus refuses to match our preconceptions of Him?

7. Whose personality or traits do you think you reflect? Can you think of any ways that Mark's Gospel may reflect Peter's personality (as tradition holds)?

8. Can you remember a time when you intentionally omitted information? Is that automatically being deceptive? Share. (Note how and why Mark omits "law.")

9. How is Paul's final appraisal (cp. II Tim. 4:11 with Acts 15:37-40) of Mark an encouragement to you? Do you know someone who is an example of the Gospel of the second (or hundreth) chance? What is he or she like?

CHAPTER 2

A. A Need-hook

Let small groups discuss what society would be like without garbage collectors. Have one person from each group share the group's thoughts. From that discussion move to a discussion of service roles various people have in our society. Finally, talk about why Jesus was the ultimate Servant.

B. Fun Features

1. Select three individuals during the week before class to do library research on the various namesakes of world religions (Mohammed, Buddha, Confucius, etc.). Let each researcher present a three-minute report on the claims of one religious leader. After the report let the group compare and contrast those leaders with Jesus' claims.

2. Let each student tell about his or her grodiest (i.e., grubbiest) job. (Usually this will have a lighthearted tinge to it.) From these stories move to the fact that the Universe Maker assumed the role of a servant (foot washing, etc.).

3. Someone could plan to rehash Mark Twain's *The Prince and the Pauper,* relating this to Jesus as Servant.

C. For Group Discussion

1. John Hick (*The Myth of God Incarnate*) believes that Jesus may have thought of Himself as a human messiah, but that the church made a mythical Son of God out of Him. How would you answer this assertion?

2. Give an example of a word (like "trunk" or "ball") that can have a totally different meaning depending upon the context. (From there discuss how "son of God" is used in the Bible.)

3. What do you think we mean when we call Jesus the "son [or Son]" of God? How would you explain this to a ten-year-old?

4. What was special about Jesus' baptism? Did your baptism have any special meaning for you? Share.

5. Which one of Jesus' three temptations (Mt. 4:1-11) means the most to you? If both the Spirit and devil were involved at Jesus' temptation, what might a Christian expect? What is your experience in dealing with an overglamorized portrayal of Christian expectations?

6. If Jesus was God's Son, how do you explain Mark 13:32? Does it teach you anything about combining psychological security with claiming ignorance?

7. What is one example of real servanthood you have seen

131

demonstrated? In what aspect do you feel you could be a better servant of the Lord?

8. (Read the illustrations of Wayne Lowe and Bob Schneider.) In what way can Christians in leadership positions (e.g., manager, executive, pastor, professor, etc.) prove to be truly servants?

CHAPTER 3

A. A Need-hook

Let class members think about a time that they felt caught in a tense situation between two opposing parties. Have them share aloud the situation and their feelings in it before turning to Matthew's seeming tightrope walk in a world of Jews (of which he was one) and Romans (for whom he worked). Share verses from both the Jews-only (e.g., Mt. 15:24) and universal (Mt. 28:18-20) strands of teaching in Matthew's Gospel.

B. Fun Features

1. Let class members discuss the matter of "atmosphere." What creates atmosphere in a particular restaurant? Why do people say, "I don't like the atmosphere of that church"? From the class discussion shift to Matthew's elements of Old Testament atmosphere.

2. Let small groups make up mock TV ads for the JRS (Jewish Revenue Service) of which Matthew was a part (e.g., "Give till it hurts").

3. If you have two class hams, let them roleplay Matthew (pro-Roman) and Simon the Zealot (anti-Roman) in a conversation when Jesus sent His disciples out two by two.

C. For Group Discussion

1. Western missionaries in the past were often guilty of squelching other cultures' styles (e.g., African or Latin American music styles) by mistakenly confusing them with something essentially Christian. Matthew's Jewishness certainly comes through in his gospel. What are some cultural insights that might be healthily used by Christians you know to further the Gospel? How do we distinguish between what's Christian and cultural? (You may wish to read and include excerpts from Don Richardson's *Eternity in Their Hearts*, Regal Books.)

2. How do you relate to the characters in the parable in Matthew 18:21-35?

3. How does Matthew (in 8:8-13 and 15:21-28) show a bigger-than-our-race Jesus?

4. What are the implications of Matthew 9:13 for your church in your community?

5. (Read the Garrison Keillor illustration, page 31, aloud.) Have your ever felt the tweezer-tear of this dilemma? When?

6. How can we be involved in the Great Commission (Mt. 28:18-20)?

7. (Read the closing illustration about David Livingstone and Matthew 28:20.) Share an occasion when such promises as "I am with you always" have stood you in good stead.

CHAPTER 4

A. A Need-hook

Matthew helped Jews of his day come to terms with their long ingrained perceptions of Messiah and revise their views. Let class members talk about how as Christians they can help those of other religious persuasions come to terms with who Jesus is and revise their views. What are some practical do's and don't's?

B. Fun Features

1. Let small groups race against each other to compile a list of cities, towns, mountains, and rivers in your country that possess Biblical names (e.g., Zion, Carmel, Bethlehem, etc.). After the game move to the material's discussion of Toledo and Matthew 1:1.

2. Let groups play Sermon on the Mount trivia. The group of three people who guesses the most quotations or general ideas in Matthew's Sermon on the Mount gets the prize (of your choosing).

C. For Group Discussion

1. Renan called Matthew the most important book ever written. Do you agree with him or not? Why or why not?

2. (Read aloud the alternating arrangement of Matthew's chapters on words and works.) What lessons can we learn from this alternating arrangement of words and works?

3. Who are the interesting characters in your own family tree? Glance over Matthew 1. Who do you find interesting in Jesus' royal family tree and why? What do these interesting people teach us?

4. Can you think of an occasion when you felt attacked (like Jesus 4:3, 6 with 3:17) at your very point of strength? What was it like?

5. How can our righteousness surpass "that of the Pharisees" (Mt. 5:20)? How can we be "perfect" (Mt. 5:48)?

6. Do you think Matthew 5:39-42 is to be taken literally? How would you practice these verses?

7. Matthew 8 and 9 is a recital of miracles. Do you think we should expect miracles? Why or why not?

8. What do you think Matthew 20:1-16 teaches, and how can we practice it? What might be some erroneous applications of it?

9. (Read part of Matthew 23 aloud.) If you didn't know this was Jesus speaking in Matthew 23, what would you think of this person? Have you ever heard a Christian talk like this? Why might we steer clear of such confrontation?

CHAPTER 5

A. A Need-hook

1. Let four people each tell a familiar story passed on by one of their family members. Why do they remember these family stories? What purpose or value do stories serve? From this discussion move to Jesus' unforgettable parables.

2. Ask students to share good and bad memories concerning medical doctors (e.g., "When I looked up the side effects of the pills he'd prescribed in a reference book, I discovered one of the side effects of that pill was the very symptom I had complained to him about").

From these stories turn to how Luke's medical background shines through his gospel, particularly in Luke 8:43 with Mark 5:26.

B. Fun Feature

Let students divide into groups of five. Each group can choose either the Parable of the Good Samaritan (Lk. 10:25-37) or the Parable of the Prodigal Son (Lk. 15). Each group must rewrite their parable in no more than ten minutes as a modern story in a modern setting. Share the stories.

C. For Group Discussion

1. How do you think Luke felt as (probably) the one Gentile writer of a New Testament document? Have you had an occasion when you were the only Christian from your (denominational, ethnic, economic, etc.) background within some larger group? How did you feel?

2. What kind of a distinctive contribution do you think a doctor could make in presenting Christ's life? What kind of contribution can you (in your job or life situation) make in passing on Christianity?

3. Can you think of any parables where Jesus may have extracted His truth right out of actual daily happenings? What can we learn from this approach? What mundane happening have you learned some truth from recently?

4. When was the last time you witnessed something that might have been an update of the Good Samaritan parable?

5. In Luke 10:25, 26 why do you think Jesus didn't just tell him the answer? Can you recall an occasion when it would have been better to withhold information for a while? Explain.

6. What does the answer of the law expert in Luke 10:37 show us about human nature?

7. Share about a time when you "came to your senses" (Lk. 15:17).

8. In what ways are you like the prodigal or the elder brother in the parable? Why is this story considered great literature?

CHAPTER 6

A. A Need-hook

Suppose someone asked you: "Do you really need a prayer life?" Or: "Why do you keep going to church? What do you get out of it?" How would you reply? From this discussion go on to Luke's treatment of spiritual exercises (e.g., the Temple, prayer, etc.).

B. Fun Features

1. Let groups of three individuals brainstorm the statement, "Prayer is like . . . ." Have them fill in the blank in as many ways as they can. They should not worry about strict confinements. It is a free association exercise to expand our insights about prayer. Let a representative read each group's similes.

2. Invite a couple of "old-timers" from your church to come and share at the outset about memories, deepening experiences, etc., that made their church experience meaningful.

From there you could switch to: "In Luke 2 we find a couple of folks—Simeon and Anna—who obviously cherished their associations with their place of worship."

C. For Group Discussion

1. What do you think are the pros and cons to a close attachment to a place of worship?

2. In Luke 19:45ff. Jesus ran salespeople out of the Temple precincts. What descriptive words or phrases would you use to imagine Jesus' presence there? What are some occasions when you think direct confrontation is called for?

3. Do you think praise affects us or God more? Why? Do you recall any memorable experiences of praising God?

4. What is your favorite Christian song or hymn? Can you think of

any particular outstanding hymn lines? What are some things that make a hymn meaningful? Why do you think Mary's song in Luke 1:46-53 reflects Hannah's prayer in I Samuel 2:1-10 so strongly?

5. Simeon felt released from his spiritual sentinel duty in Luke 2:29. Have you ever felt that there was one particular spiritual "assignment" or project that you had to take care of? Share the circumstances.

6. What emotions would have run through your mind if you had been Mary and just been told about your supernatural pregnancy? Has anyone you know found himself or herself in an unusual predicament due to his or her faith commitment? What happened?

7. John the Baptist was "filled with the Holy Spirit even from birth" (Lk. 1:15). How would you expect a Spirit-filled child to act?

8. Have you ever felt that something you said (cf. Lk. 12:12) on a special occasion might be attributed to the Holy Spirit's help? How did you know?

CHAPTER 7

A. A Need-hook

Have your class share illustrations of how someone within their awareness was hurt (e.g., name-calling, injustice, etc.) simply because of their racial, economic, sexual, or social background. This is obviously a sensitive subject so it will need to be handled with sensitivity.

From this discussion move to how Luke shows great awareness of women, the poor, outcasts, Gentiles, Samaritans, etc.

B. Fun Features

1. Let small groups imagine they are a restaurant waiter or taxicab driver on a tourist island where there is also considerable poverty. Let a group representative jot down the imagined server's thoughts about a swanky American tourist he is serving. Encourage creativity in this exercise and let group representatives share their group's results with the whole class.

2. Ask ahead of time two of the class members to stage an eight-minute debate on "The Christian message is spiritual and private" versus "The Christian message is social and public." Humor is permissible from the debaters who could take turns speaking twice for two minutes each.

C. For Group Discussion

1. How did God defy our expectations in the birth of Jesus? If Jesus had

been middle class, how do you suppose He would have been born?

2. How do you think you would feel if you had been born missing one ear? How do you think you would have learned to cope? How do you think such a person feels when they are taught as children to sing, "I'm so happy and here's the reason why" Or "Happiness is the Lord"?

3. How would you evaluate the statement: "Christianity is not a social gospel"?

4. Luke names at least 13 women not found in the other Gospels. Do you think the local church is meeting the needs of women today? If there were to be some change, what would you like to see?

5. If you were Jewish, how would you want to be treated by a Gentile Christian?

6. Why do you think Jesus didn't "leave well enough alone" when He had a good thing going at Nazareth (Lk. 4:22 compared with 4:24-29)? Cite some cases where God seemed to shun the racially smug and shower His blessings elsewhere.

7. What can we do to sensitize Christians more about labeling someone with a handicap or physical difference (Lk. 6:6; 19:3)?

8. Is it apparent that Christians we know love "sinners" (i.e., of the variety Jesus did)? If not, how can we improve? What could your group do about this in a concrete, action-oriented way?

CHAPTER 8

A. A Need-hook

Have class members brainstorm all the things that give *structure* to their lives (e.g., school bells ringing, curbs on streets, guardrails on mountains, traffic signals, the human skeleton, etc.). Ask: what would be some of the implications of life without structure? Turn then to the strong sense of structure in the Gospel of John, i.e., the organizational features of seven signs and seven sayings. A still deeper structure resides in Jesus' "I am" claims.

B. Fun Features

1. Let class members race one another in small groups by naming or drawing as many signs (street, highway, etc.) as they can.

2. Let class members race one another in small groups by compiling a list of as many holidays or red-letter days as they can.

C. For Group Discussion

1. How do Jesus' miracles in John's Gospel present Him as the Need-meeter? What neighborhood, community, or personal needs are you

currently aware of? How could those needs be addressed?

2. What would you do tomorrow if today you had miraculously straightened out a woman's broken arm? What do you think the purpose of miracles is?

3. (Read John 2:13-17 and 7:37-39 aloud.) What animal might Jesus make you think of when looking at the aspects of Him revealed in these two passages? Why do you think of that animal?

4. What do you think "I am the bread of life" (Jn. 6:34) means to us whose refrigerator is stocked—and perhaps even the breadbox contains rye, pumpernickel, etc.?

5. If Jesus were to proclaim an "I am . . ." from things distinctively a part of our modern world, what do you think He might say He was?

6. If you were to draw a picture of *misery*, what would you draw? Which of Jesus' seven "I am"s do you think best satisfies that need?

7. Jesus could say clearly and pictorially who He was ("I am . . ."). If you were asked, "Who are you?" (and you could not reply by stating your name or job), what would you say?

8. How is Jesus' proclamation, "I am the resurrection and the life" (Jn. 11:25), most meaningful to you?

CHAPTER 9

A. A Need-hook

Let students try to think of instances when they believed in someone (no names, please), but their belief was disappointed because of the person's unreliability. After the class stories, contrast the fact that we rely upon Jesus' reliability for eternal life.

B. Fun Features

1. Ask students to sit without talking until you give the word. People discover quickly this way how hard it is just to keep looking at other human beings without saying anything. Probably a few giggles will arise. Let the silence go on and on . . . and on for a while. Time yourself, so you can observe that it was only two minutes (or whatever) of silence—that seemed like an *eternity*. Explore futher by asking: "When I say 'eternity,' what ideas come to your mind?"

2. Ask students to share any amusing or better-forgotten tales on the subject of "witnessing" (Christian or otherwise).

C. For Group Discussion

1. What are some other synonyms for "to believe" or "to have faith"? In what ways is Christian commitment like a good marriage?

2. In what sense is faith active and in what sense is it passive?

3. Share a witnessing experience with the group. What things are either attractive or unattractive about the witness various Christians give?

4. How do you evaluate the statement: "It's not what you believe, but whom you believe"? Or evaluate: "Creeds just give you a paper Christ."

5. God calls Christians His "children." In what sense are we to be like or unlike children (childlike—I Cor. 14:20; Eph. 4:14)?

6. How would you answer the argument of modern scholars that the early church took the simple man Jesus and turned Him into a God?

7. How would you complete the following statement: If Jesus Christ is God, then we . . .?

8. What does Jesus having a physical body (Jn. 1:14) have to say to us about our physicalness?

9. What do you understand is meant in the KJV by the expression "only begotten" Son? (Leader: See the chapter material here for gauging your answers.)

10. How is eternal life meaningful to you in the present?

CHAPTER 10

A. A Need-hook

Invite class members to share a time when they found it difficult to be both loving and truthful at the same time. (P.S. Sometimes it's best to call on quieter members by name so as to prevent the same people from doing all the talking.) After sharing, move to John's themes of truth and love.

B. Fun Features

1. Make up your own series of crazy questions along the lines of the old show "Truth or Consequences." (e.g., "What is the first four-headed thing in the Bible?" [Buzzer sounds. Read answer from Genesis 2:10 in KJV.] "Sorry. Because you didn't tell the truth, you must pay the consequences, so you'll have to tell us your most embarrassing memory." From there shift to John's treatment of truth.

2. Let class members share any childhood memories concerning light and darkness before referring to light in John's Gospel.

C. For Group Discussion

1. How do you answer the claim that believing Jesus' statement, "I am the way and the truth," makes you intolerant? What do you think

intolerance is? How does one approach someone from some other religious persuasion?

2. (Read aloud the two paragraphs beginning with "When the famed Dead Sea scrolls . . ." on page 95.) How can we slip into the trap of being more like the people at Qumran than like Jesus? What situations have you seen that illustrate this problem?

3. What is your favorite truth about (or picture of) the Holy Spirit? What emotions rise up in you when people speak of the Spirit? Why that emotion?

4. How does a Christian relate to the Holy Spirit as a person within? Does He just do things automatically to change you (say a habit) when you pray?

5. In what ways is the Spirit of God like a paramedic or lawyer to you?

6. How do you think a Christian tells if he or she is placing too much or too little emphasis upon the work of the Spirit?

7. Can you think of an example of unselfish or self-sacrificing love within your circle of family or friends? Share.

8. Jesus asked Peter if he loved Him "more than these" (Jn. 21:15), i.e., friends, boats, etc. What clues help Christians tell when they have elevated things (home, possessions, etc.) too high in their sense of priorities?

CHAPTER 11

A. A Need-hook

Let the class discuss how they would answer some of the four problems raised in the chapter's introduction.

B. Fun Features

1. Let the class play the game of telephone: whispering a single sentence (without repeating it) around the circle of people. (Normally the original sentence will turn out laughably different than the message that arrived at the last ear.) From that exercise, lead into the question of how the Christian message had to be preserved truthfully during the approximately 20 years between Jesus' resurrection and the first written New Testament documents.

2. Let class members share family traditions (laughable or serious) that have been passed on to them. Then talk about the early oral traditions of Christianity that were faithfully "passed on" (I Cor. 15:3 ff.; II Thess. 2:15) prior to the written New Testament.

C. For Group Discussion

1. William Barclay said on I John 2:18—"In fact John was wrong" (*The Letters of John and Jude*, p. 60). What do you think of Barclay's statement? If the Bible is wrong on some point, how would one decide what is true and what is an error in it?

2. Most Bible scholars assume that Matthew used the earlier Mark's Gospel. (Read the class the reasons for thinking this.) If this is so, why might an eyewitness and apostle (Matthew) use the material of one who was not an apostle (Mark)?

3. Paul held a "pattern of sound teaching" (II Tim. 1:13). What items would you include in your own core of Christian belief? Why do these items seem essential to you?

4. Compare some erroneous teachings that arose within New Testament times and churches (II Tim. 2:17, 18; I Jn. 2:18-27; 4:1-3). What are some religious errors today of which you are aware? What are some practical or ethical errors?

5. Read and compare Matthew 27:37; Mark 15:26; Luke 23:38; and John 19:19. What becomes apparent from the reading of the four superscriptions? Therefore, what understanding should we have of how the gospel writers report Jesus' words and works?

6. Have you ever discovered something in the four Gospels that seemed contradictory? What was it? How did you deal with it?

8. Can you give an example of a cultural difference from the Western world and the Eastern world of the Bible? Have you ever had to act differently because of someone else's customs (e.g., in-laws)? What did it teach you?

CHAPTER 12

A. A Need-hook

Ask your class if they've ever been in a car accident or court case where there was more than one witness. What did the varying viewpoints contribute? (You may go on from there to discuss modern reports with varying viewpoints, such as President Kennedy's death or the Gary Dotson retrial.) Let the class see how many reasons they can think of for more than one gospel.

B. Fun Features

1. Pass out pencils and papers, and let your class all draw an arrangement of a pile of tools stacked up in the middle of the room. Have them show their masterpieces with the individual differences.

Shift to a discussion of four portraits of Jesus (and the analogy of four famous painters used in the chapter) in the Gospels.

2. Let the class look for one minute at a fairly complicated picture or wall painting. Take the picture away and ask them to write out in two minutes what they remember from the picture. Following this, discuss the fact that the Gospels were probably all written over 20 years after the events took place!

C. For Group Discussion

1. Matthew and Mark's Gospels are very similar. How would you compare them to two animals, cars, flowers, etc.?

2. What favorite story, event, or teaching helps you remember or capsule one of the four Gospels? How do you identify with that remembrance? Who do you know who exemplifies one important theme from the Gospels?

3. Do you remember any incidents or teachings only found in John's Gospel? (If not, read the list of "onlies" to them.) What do you relate to best from this list and why?

4. What practical lessons can the variedness in the four Gospels teach us?

5. Matthew seems to be an ethnically targeted Gospel. What are the strengths and weaknesses of a church ministering to a fairly homogenous group of people?

6. Mark seems to have been something of an impulsive, rapid-acting person. What are the pros and cons of such behavior? Do you find yourself frequently acting too quickly or slowly? Share.

7. Luke mingles the spiritual and social together. Which aspect in your life do you feel could use the most beefing up? Why?

8. What pleasant memory do you think you'll take away from this course? What has spoken to you most particularly?